you are™
what
you eat

you are what you eat™

Shop. Eat.
Quick and Easy

Carina Norris

First published in Great Britain in 2007 by
Virgin Books Ltd
Thames Wharf Studios
Rainville Road
London
W6 9HA

A catalogue record for this book is available from the British Library.

ISBN 978 0 7535 1290 6

The paper used in this book is a natural, recyclable product made from wood grown in
sustainable forests. The manufacturing process conforms to the regulations of the country of
origin.

Any content and/or facts and/or advice included in this book is intended as a guide only and
should not be used as an alternative to seeking professional advice from either your doctor or
a registered specialist for yourself or for anyone else. If you are displaying any symptoms or
illness that concern you, especially if you are pregnant, infirm, elderly or under 16 years of age,
we recommend you consult a doctor or a registered specialist at the earliest opportunity.

Designed by Virgin Books Ltd

Printed and bound in Great Britain by The Bath Press

Photography © Shutterstock

Contents

Introduction 6

Chapter 1   Shopping 14

Chapter 2   Cooking 38

Chapter 3   Eating on the move 54

Chapter 4   Healthy lunches for
             grown-ups and kids 80

Chapter 5   Let's celebrate! 102

Introduction

SHOPPING AND EATING MADE EASY

Here it is, the first *You Are What You Eat™* pocket book, the ultimate quick and easy guide to healthy eating for keeping your body fit and strong and your mind stable and contented. By picking up this book, you've shown that you care about what you eat. Good for you!

This book is all about making your life easier. It will show you how to fill your kitchen full of tasty, healthy foods. You won't be asked to spend hours in the kitchen or spend a fortune on exotic or elusive ingredients. This book is realistic, understands the pressures of work, family and relationships, and won't set you impossible goals.

It's all about making healthy eating easy, convenient, enjoyable and, above all, practical.

Here's what you'll find inside this book:

- The **nutritional know-how** to make healthy food choices
- At-a-glance **checklists** to make healthy food shopping a breeze
- How to read the **labels** – and not be fooled by the manufacturers' ploys
- Tips for **calmer cooking** – keep stress out of the kitchen
- Advice on the healthiest **cooking methods**
- What to choose when **eating away from home,** from travel snacks and holiday meals to takeaways and parties
- What to pack and choose without sacrificing your healthy lifestyle when it comes to **packed lunches and work canteens**
- A **celebration survival guide** – Christmas, New Year and birthdays needn't spell doom for healthy eating

The benefits of healthy eating can be all yours – bags of energy, clearer skin, shinier hair, better circulation, fewer minor illnesses and improved all-round health.

And, by eating the You Are What You Eat way, you could also add years to your life – healthy food reduces your risk of diseases such as cancer, heart disease and stroke. It can even reduce your risk of Alzheimer's, and reduce the natural age-related slowing down of the brain.

Although this book isn't a weight-loss manual, it can help you shed excess pounds. If your diet's a mess now, and you're keeping yourself going between meals with sugary or fatty snacks, you'll almost certainly be piling in the calories. And, if you're not active enough, that's a sure recipe for weight gain.

By switching to healthier foods you can lose weight naturally and gradually, because not only are the kinds of foods we recommend higher in important nutrients than the 'junk' options, but they generally contain fewer calories. By eating healthy whole foods such as fruit, vegetables and tasty grains you'll feel full for longer, and be less likely to grab a chocolate muffin or a stack of biscuits. By eating the correct amount of nutritious food, you'll help your body weight to stabilise at the healthy level – for you.

We'll show you how to regain control of your eating, and your life!

10 STEPS TO A HEALTHIER LIFESTYLE

When you replace the fatty, sugary, processed junk in your diet with tasty, fresh whole foods (plenty of fresh fruit and vegetables, for example, and low-fat protein foods such as fish, and sustaining whole grains) you'll be giving your body the fuel it needs, rather than junk that will clog it up and slow it down.

For now, all you need are a few simple guidelines. Follow these, and you'll soon be eating healthily. They may look daunting – but don't panic! Change just one bad eating habit and you're on your way. Start with baby steps – you don't need giant leaps in order to see progress.

1. *Get the breakfast habit*

Never skip breakfast, or else by mid-morning you'll feel sluggish and irritable. A filling, nourishing breakfast sustains your energy, and helps you to resist sugary snacks.

2. *Keep hydrated*

Your body contains approximately 65 per cent water. Even mild dehydration can make you weak, dizzy and lacking in energy.

Try to drink 1.5–2 litres of water a day (about 8–10 glasses) – build up to your target gradually.

Pure water is by far the best source of fluids for hydration, but you can also boost your fluid intake with herbal and fruit teas or diluted fruit juice. Avoid fizzy drinks and squash – they're packed with sugar and sweeteners.

3. *Get fresh!*

The fresher your food, the more nutrients it will contain. The vitamin content of fruit and vegetables begins to decline from the moment they are harvested. Try, if you can, to shop for fresh food little and often.

Look for homegrown fruit and vegetables when they're in season, and buy from pick-your-own growers, farm shops and farmers' markets.

Check the sell-by dates on packaged fruit and vegetables and try to buy and use them as far before the dates as you can.

If you buy organic, you'll get fewer chemicals such as pesticides on fruit and vegetables, and fewer hormones, antibiotics and growth promoters in meat, milks and eggs.

Try growing your own herbs, vegetables and salads.

4. *Make it yourself*

Ditch the processed-food habit! Processed foods are generally packed with salt, sugar and saturated and hydrogenated (so-called *trans*) fats – all nutritional baddies. They're also often loaded with bulkers, fillers and additives with no nutritional value.

If you prepare and cook your own food from scratch, you'll know exactly what went into it.

5. *Eat five a day – at least!*

The World Health Organisation says we should all be eating at least five portions of fruit and vegetables a day – and with good reason. Fruit and vegetables are rich in vitamins and minerals, fibre, carbohydrates and beneficial phytochemicals. They also have many health benefits, including lowered risk for certain cancers, stroke, heart disease and high blood pressure. And if five a day is good, more is even better!

6. *Send the deep-fat fryer packing!*

Avoid deep-fat frying, and when you do fry any food, use only a tiny quantity of oil and cook for a short period of time, as in stir-frying. Use olive, corn, sunflower or rapeseed oil.

7. *Eat good fats*

Not all fats are bad – you just need to choose wisely. All fats are high in calories, so can cause weight gain if you eat too much of them. But monounsaturated fats and polyunsaturated fats have health benefits, and our bodies need a certain amount of them.

We need to cut down on the bad fats while ensuring that we have enough of the good fats.

Know your fats

Saturated fats: These raise your cholesterol levels, clog your arteries and increase your heart-disease risk. They're generally solid at room temperature, and are found in animal products (meat, eggs, dairy products) and 'tropical oils' such as coconut and palm oil.

Trans fats: Trans fats are found in hydrogenated or partially hydrogenated vegetable oils that have undergone a hardening process to improve their keeping properties. These fats have similar harmful effects to (and slightly worse than) saturated fats.

Hydrogenated fats are used to lengthen the shelf life of many processed foods. Avoiding trans fats is yet another good reason to cook your own food!

Monounsaturated fats: Olive oil, canola oil, peanut oil and also avocados are high in monounsaturates. Olive and canola oils (small quantities, of course) are the best for frying, since they are less susceptible to being damaged by heat and forming harmful compounds.

Polyunsaturated fats: Safflower oil, sunflower oil and corn oil are all good sources of polyunsaturates. Omega-3 and omega-6 fatty acids are kinds of polyunsaturates, found in oily fish, nuts and seeds, which help lower cholesterol levels, reduce our heart-disease risk and even benefit our mood.

8. *Cut down sugar*

Most people eat far too much sugary food, which can contribute to obesity and tooth decay, as well as crowding out more nutritious foods from our diets. Sugar provides instant energy, but its effect is short-lived and we soon crave more sweet things.

The body doesn't need pure sugar for fuel – it's better to get energy from the natural sugars in fruits, and by breaking down starchy carbohydrates and even protein and fats. Sugar in sweets, biscuits and other sugary processed food may taste good, but it has little to recommend it. Swap your sugary snack for a piece of fruit, a handful of dried fruit or a wholemeal currant bun or scone.

9. *Reduce the salt*

Salt can contribute to high blood pressure, increasing our risk of heart disease and stroke. Many of us have too much salt, especially if we eat a lot of processed foods. Wean yourself off adding salt at the table, add less in cooking, and – most importantly – cut down the amount of processed food you serve.

10. *Make more of wholefoods*

Beans and lentils are full of cholesterol-lowering soluble fibre and packed with protein, making them a healthy and delicious alternative to meat and animal products, which are higher in fat, particularly the 'bad' saturated fat.

And have wholemeal bread, pasta and rice instead of white, and try some of the other tasty grains, such as bulghar, buckwheat, millet and quinoa.

Wholemeal and 'brown' foods are in their natural, most nutritious state. When they're processed to make 'white' foods, they lose much of their nutritional value.

Chapter One
Shopping

you are™
what
you eat

LOOK AND THINK BEFORE YOU BUY!

This should be your motto for healthy shopping.

- Check the salt, fat (especially saturated fat) and sugar content – most of us eat far more than we need.
- Check the ingredients – look at the label to see that products are not packed full of additives, E-numbers and colours.
- Check the country of origin of items you buy – would you rather have a lettuce from a field ten miles up the road or one that had travelled halfway around the world to reach the supermarket, losing nutrients along the way?
- Check the ingredients list to see there is nothing you are trying to avoid – such as hydrogenated vegetable fats (the source of unhealthy trans fats), or an ingredient someone in your family is allergic or sensitive to. Most supermarket chains have recently phased out the use of trans fats in their own-brand products.
- Check that the product is in good condition.
- Check use-by and best-before dates.

HEALTHY SHOPPING

- Hunt out your local street markets, specialist food shops, farm shops, farmers' markets and pick-your-own outlets for fresh fruit and vegetables.
- Always buy fruit and vegetables in small quantities – you will have less waste and they will be fresher, and therefore higher in nutrients.
- Keep a few tins of beans and pulses in your cupboard so you can make quick and nutritious stews, casseroles and bakes.

- Stock up with wholemeal or semi-wholemeal pasta and spaghetti to create quick suppers and lunches.
- Make friends with your butcher and fishmonger. Many supermarkets now have fresh meat and fish counters where you can buy exactly what you need, and get advice on how to prepare and cook it.

A healthier shopping basket

Buy more:
- fresh fruit and vegetables
- nuts and seeds
- brown rice and wholemeal pasta
- pulses – lentils and beans
- skimmed milk, low-fat fromage frais and low-fat yoghurt
- wholemeal bread and rolls
- skinless chicken and turkey
- oily fish – salmon, fresh tuna, sardines, pilchards, trout etc.

Buy less/fewer:
- meat and meat products
- processed and ready meals
- cream, full-fat milk and full-fat yoghurt
- butter and cheese
- fatty chips and crisps
- biscuits and cakes
- sweets and chocolate

Vegetables	Which to buy
Cabbages	The outer leaves should be crisp, not yellowed, the heart should be firm and the stem clean and firm.
Beans	Should be firm and not limp or bendy. Tips should not be blackened.
Onions	Should be firm, the outer skins dry, and should not have sprouted.
Lettuces	Should be crisp and have no yellow or slimy leaves.
Tomatoes	Check they are firm and undamaged.
Cucumbers	Should be firm along the whole length with no black spots or soft areas.
Asparagus	The tips should be firm and dry and the stalks plump and unwrinkled.
Cauliflower	Should be white and firm with no black or brown speckled areas.
Potatoes	Should not have started to sprout and should have no green patches on them.
Carrots	Should be plump and not wizened and have no black spots.
Courgettes and marrows	Should have no dark soft patches and be firm. Some varieties have pale-green or yellow skins and others have dark-green skins.
Mushrooms	Should be firm, dry and clean.

Fruits	Which to buy
Oranges	Should be firm and have no soft spots or patches of white mould. They should feel heavy for their size.
Bananas	If you want them to last, select those that are green and they will continue to ripen at home. Don't store them with other kinds of fruit.
Lemons	Should be firm and unblemished and feel heavy for their size.
Apples	Should be firm and not wrinkled.
Grapes	Should be dry and unwrinkled. If grapes fall off the bunch when you shake it gently, they are overripe.
Melons	Should be firm without any soft patches or dark spots.
Pineapples	Should be firm, with no soft or black patches. A pineapple is ripe when a leaf can be simply pulled out from the top.
Cherries	Should be plump and dry.
Strawberries	Should be firm with no evidence of leaking juice or of mould.
Pears	Should be firm, with no soft areas, bruising or blemishes.
Mangoes	Should be firm (but not too hard), slightly fragrant, and have no black marks on the skin.

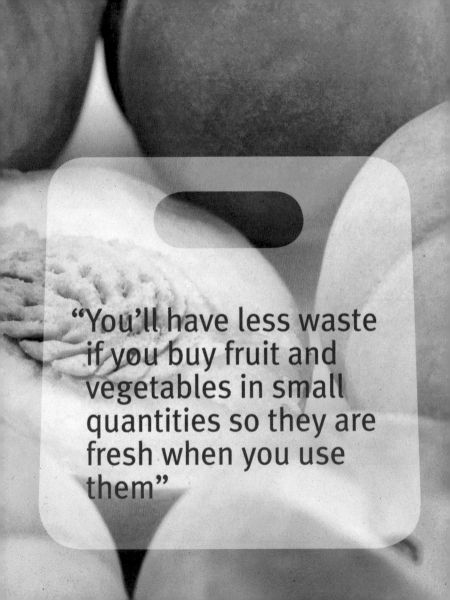

"You'll have less waste if you buy fruit and vegetables in small quantities so they are fresh when you use them"

READING THE LABELS

Become a label sleuth – once you can decipher the food labels, you won't be taken in by any overhyped marketing claims.

- Foods labelled 'low in sugar' are often packed with fat, and those 'low in fat' are often high in sugar.
- Many breakfast cereals are fortified with vitamins, but these artificially added vitamins could be harder for the body to absorb than vitamins naturally found in food. Some breakfast cereals – even the wholegrain ones – are also alarmingly high in sugar and salt.
- 'No added sugar' doesn't necessarily mean the food is totally virtuous as far as sweetenings are concerned. Although any sweetness may come from natural fruit sugars (which are much better for us than refined sugar), the product may contain artificial sweeteners.
- Foods with 'No artificial preservatives' may still contain natural preservatives such as salt or sugar.
- 'Reduced-calorie' simply means it contains fewer calories than the regular version – it may still be high in calories itself. A good example is 'reduced-calorie crisps'.

Ingredients are listed in descending order, with the main ingredient first in the list.

Most manufactured foods have a table showing nutrients per portion, and per 100g, and the Food Standards Agency has produced these guidelines to help us to avoid the 'baddies' in our food.

This is *a lot* per 100g food:
- 20g fat or more
- 5g saturates (saturated fat) or more
- 0.5g sodium or more
- 10g sugars or more

This is *a little* per 100g food:
- 3g fat or less
- 1g saturates or less
- 0.1g sodium or less
- 2g sugars or less

You should also try to avoid trans (hydrogenated and partially hydrogenated) fats, since they have similar effects to (and possibly worse than) saturated fats on our cholesterol levels and risk of heart disease.

HEALTH CLAIMS

Now that more people are learning the benefits of a healthy diet, the food companies are keen to lure us in with health and nutritional claims, such as 'low in fat', 'a source of fibre' or 'promotes heart health'. But it can be difficult to figure out just how healthy all of these foods are. Until recently, the law governing these claims was very lax, full of loopholes and with lots of room for manufacturers to interpret the guidelines in different ways.

Fortunately, new European Union legislation being introduced is tightening up the loopholes. For example, foods won't be able to make any actual health claims, such as 'reduces cholesterol' or 'good for your heart' if they are high in unhealthy ingredients such as fat, salt and sugar. For example, the label on a yoghurt drink won't be allowed to say it's good for your bones, even though it's high in bone-healthy calcium, if it's also packed with unhealthy added sugars.

However, at the time of writing, companies have been given until 2009 to conform to all of the new rules. The new legislation also tightens up the definitions of descriptions, and includes those below:

Low-calorie:	No more than 40kcal/100g for foods, or 20kcal/100ml for drinks.
Reduced-calorie:	30% fewer calories than the 'standard' version.
Reduced-sugar:	30% less sugar than the 'standard' version.
Low-sugar:	No more than 5g sugars per 100g for foods. No more than 2.5g sugars per 100ml for drinks.
No added sugars:	Must not contain added sugars. If sugar is naturally found in that food, the label must say, 'contains naturally occurring sugars'.
Reduced-fat:	30% less fat than the 'standard' version.

Low fat:	No more than 3g fat per 100g for solid foods. No more than 1.5g fat per 100ml for liquids (1.8g fat for semiskimmed milk).
Low sodium/low salt:	No more than 0.12g sodium per 100g or 100ml. No more than 0.3g salt per 100g or 100ml.
Very low sodium/very low salt:	No more than 0.04g sodium per 100g or 100ml. No more than 0.1g salt per 100g or 100ml.
Source of fibre:	At least 3g fibre per 100g or at least 1.5g fibre per 100kcal. No more than 0.4kcal/portion equivalent to 1 tsp sugar, for tabletop sweeteners.
High fibre:	Must contain at least 6g fibre per 100g or at least 3g fibre per 100kcal.

(Note, incidentally, that 'kcal' means kilocalories, or what we would normally just call calories. Except in strictly scientific usage, both are the same.)

When all's said and done, the 'best' ingredients lists are the shortest ones, with words you recognise, rather than all those E numbers and unpronounceable chemicals. And whole foods *without* ingredients lists – such as fresh vegetables and fruit – are better still!

Reading labels for salt

Many labels list sodium rather than salt – this is because sodium is the harmful constituent of salt.

- One gram of sodium is the equivalent of 2.5g salt, so if a label lists the sodium content, multiply it by 2.5 to get the salt content. This means that a portion of food with 0.5g sodium actually contains 1.25g of salt – well on the way to the maximum recommended daily intake of 6g.
- Salt lurks in a huge variety of processed foods – from tomato ketchup to cornflakes – so it's very easy to go over the limit, even if you don't add salt at the table or in your cooking.

TAKING THE STRESS OUT OF SHOPPING

Buying a shopping trolley filled with healthy foods each week needn't be too time-consuming, stressful or expensive.

Clever shopping tips

- Always go armed with a shopping list. Aimless wandering along the aisles searching for inspiration wastes time and invariably you end up with more than you need.
- Plan a week's menus before you write your list, but be prepared to amend it if you spot a bargain or special offer.
- Take advantage of special offers on foods you regularly buy.

- Group similar items together on your shopping list so you do not have to crisscross the store.
- Keep a running shopping list in the kitchen and get into the habit of jotting down items you are about to run out of. Get the rest of the family to do the same.
- Switch to supermarkets' own-brand products for items such as tinned chopped tomatoes, rice and pasta.
- Look out for fruit and vegetables when they are in season. They won't have clocked up thousands of air miles to reach the shop and are generally cheaper.
- Use money-off vouchers from magazines and newspapers.
- Check out the supermarkets' frozen-food aisles – you'll often find special offers such as buy-one-get-one-free, or large packs of chicken breasts or chops.
- Look out for new lines – they're often offered at an 'introductory' price when they first arrive on the shelves. But buy and try before you stock up – the special prices usually last a few weeks.
- Don't shop when you're hungry. Research has shown that if we shop when we are hungry we buy more.
- Keep away from the aisles you won't need. Spend your time among the fresh fruit and skip the crisps and fizzy-drinks aisles.
- Consider shopping online. You'll be less likely to impulse-buy.
- Look into ordering an organic fruit and vegetable box from a local farm or a national company.

SHOPPING IN SEASON

Buying locally produced food when it is in season will give you the best flavour and the most nutrients. And it's often less expensive.

In **spring** look for:
- cauliflowers
- new potatoes
- artichokes
- chicory
- shallots
- spring greens

In **summer** look for:
- asparagus
- broad beans
- runner beans
- dwarf beans
- new potatoes
- mange tout
- sugar-snap peas
- spinach
- courgettes
- Chinese leaves
- cucumber
- garlic
- lettuce
- runner beans
- peas
- spinach
- peppers
- tomatoes
- radishes
- apricots
- cherries
- plums
- peaches
- nectarines
- strawberries
- raspberries
- redcurrants
- blackcurrants

In **autumn** look for:
- broccoli
- Brussels sprouts
- marrow
- fennel
- cabbage
- spinach
- squash
- plums
- pears
- apples
- beetroot

In **winter** look for:
- Brussels sprouts
- winter cabbage
- cauliflower
- celery
- leeks
- onions
- parsnips
- swedes
- squash
- Jerusalem artichokes
- beetroot
- celeriac

THE HEALTHY STORE CUPBOARD

Having a healthy store cupboard will help you to eat well. There is no need to empty your cupboards of unhealthy products in one go – that would be wasteful. Just resolve not to replace the junk food and unhealthy options.

Gradually add a healthy new staple food to your shopping list each week, and buy only a small quantity until you and the family have tasted it. When you run out of white rice, replace it with brown rice; when the white pasta is finished, replace it with wholemeal.

Turn the page for some useful items to have in your store cupboard.

THE HEALTHY STORE CUPBOARD

Grains
- rice
- millet
- bulghar wheat
- buckwheat
- couscous
- oats

Nuts and seeds
- almonds
- Brazil nuts
- hazelnuts
- walnuts
- pine nuts
- cashew nuts
- pumpkin seeds
- sesame seeds
- sunflower seeds

Beans (tinned or dried) and pulses
- adzuki beans
- cannelloni beans
- red kidney beans
- chickpeas
- red lentils
- Continental lentils

Flour
- wholewheat plain and self-raising flour
- strong wholemeal bread flour
- cornflour
- rice flour

Herbs and spices
- mixed herbs
- basil
- mint
- mixed spice
- ground ginger
- cinnamon
- curry powder

Dried fruit

- raisins
- sultanas
- currants
- dried apricots (unsulphured and natural)

- dried figs
- dried cranberries and or blueberries (unsweetened)
- dried apples, prunes, peaches, pears

Tins and cartons

- tinned tomatoes
- tinned fish (salmon, sardines, mackerel, tuna)
- tinned sweetcorn
- low-sugar, low-salt baked beans

- tinned pulses such as chickpeas and red kidney beans
- long life cartons of pure juice – apple, orange

Tins of fruit in juice, and low-salt, low-sugar vegetables, in your store cupboard are useful. They may not have all the nutrient benefits of fresh or frozen, but they're better than nothing if you need them in a hurry.

Storing canned and dried food

A well-stocked store cupboard is an asset to the busy cook, but
canned and dried foods can deteriorate if they're not kept properly.

- Staples such as rice, salt, sugar, flour, pasta, dried beans, grains
  and seeds should be kept in moisture-proof containers and jars.
  In general wholegrain products keep for a shorter time than
  refined products.
- Store oil in a dark cupboard, away from heat.
- Some sauces, oils, and preserves need to be kept in the fridge
  once they have been opened. Always check the label and use
  before the use-by date.
- Always buy herbs and spices in small quantities and keep out of
  the light in a cupboard or drawer. Ground spices and chopped
  dried herbs quickly lose their flavour. When substituting
  dried herbs for fresh herbs use 1 teaspoon of dried herbs to 1
  tablespoon of fresh herbs.
- If you decant food from its packaging into canisters, always use
  the contents before adding more. Never add new food to older
  food in the container.
- Check cans often to see that none are damaged or past their eat-
  by date.

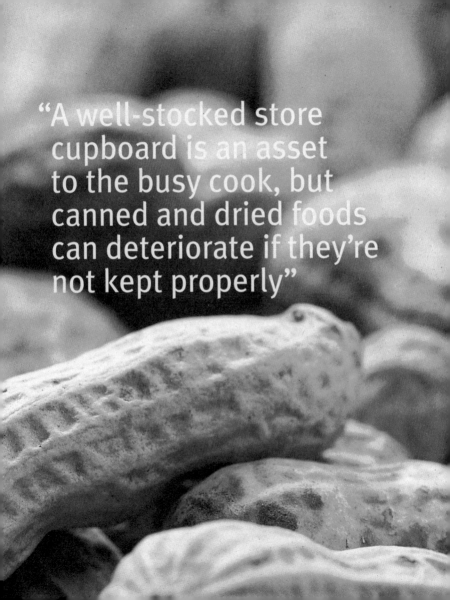

"A well-stocked store cupboard is an asset to the busy cook, but canned and dried foods can deteriorate if they're not kept properly"

WEANING FOR GROWN-UPS

Try to wean yourself on to a healthier, low-salt, low-sugar, low-fat diet. Do it gradually, and you'll hardly notice the difference.

Cutting fat

Most of us eat far more fat than our bodies need – but it's simple to cut down.

- When you're shopping, read the labels and avoid high-fat processed food, particularly if it contains a lot of saturated fat or hydrogenated fats (trans fats).
- Have at least two fish meals, one beans meal and one other vegetarian dish each week.
- Replace some of the meat content of dishes by adding beans, lentils, whole grains or extra vegetables.
- Try to replace as much of the saturated fats in your diet (found in foods such as meat and full-fat dairy products) as possible with healthy unsaturated alternatives, such as olive oil.
- Trim all visible fat from meat and remove skin from chicken and turkey before cooking.
- Don't buy burgers or sausages. Make your own burgers and replace some of the meat with finely chopped vegetables or mashed beans.
- Choose cooking methods that use little or no oil.
- Use a spray to dispense oil when you are cooking so that you can use less.
- Cut down the amount of butter or spread you use on bread and toast.
- Change from whole milk to semiskimmed or skimmed milk.

- Change to low-fat cream cheese and use half-fat hard cheese.
- Replace full-fat yoghurt with low-fat natural yoghurt sweetened with honey or fruit.
- Add semiskimmed evaporated milk instead of single cream to casseroles and stews.
- When you are making scrambled egg, use one whole egg and one egg white per person.
- Top pies with crumpled filo pastry instead of puff, flaky or shortcrust pastry.
- Use low-fat salad dressings. Make your own so you know what goes into them. A splash of balsamic vinegar on a salad is delicious.

Cutting salt

Since most of the salt in our diets comes from the increasing amount of processed food we eat, the easiest and most effective way to cut down is to eat more fresh food. A shocking 75 per cent of the salt we eat comes from manufactured foods, rather than the salt we add ourselves.

- Get into baking and make your own cakes and biscuits. Shop-bought cakes and biscuits are often high in salt.
- Make your own savoury snacks – homemade bagel crisps (see the recipe on Page 59), plain popcorn with a sprinkling of chilli powder or finely grated Parmesan.
- Supermarket ready meals are often high in salt. Give them a miss and make your own.
- Make your own soups so you can control the salt.

- Gradually reduce the amount of salt you add during cooking. Add salt near to the end of cooking time when you are cooking vegetables, and gradually add less.
- Experiment with herbs, spices and reduced-salt soy sauce, to add flavour to your cooking.
- Choose low-salt options for baked beans and tinned spaghetti.
- If you must have them, keep takeaway meals, which are often high in salt, for very occasional consumption.
- Remove the saltcellar from the dining table so you aren't tempted to add salt to your food.
- If you buy canned vegetables for emergencies, look for those canned in water, not brine.
- If you use stock cubes or bouillon powder in your cooking, look for brands that are low in salt (and free from hydrogenated vegetable oil).

Cutting sugar

A little sugar in your diet isn't bad for you. It's the *kind* of sugar and the *amount* you eat that matter. Unfortunately, most of us consume too much of the wrong kinds.

- Avoid sugar-packed breakfast cereals in favour of low-sugar, or no-added-sugar wholegrain cereals. Sweeten them with fresh or dried fruit, chopped nuts, seeds or a drizzle of honey.
- Make your own low-sugar muesli from oat flakes, nuts, seeds and dried fruit.
- Stock up on non-sugar or low-sugar toppings for toast and sandwiches. Try fruit spreads, reduced-sugar peanut butter and reduced-sugar jams.

- Buy low-sugar versions of baked beans and tinned spaghetti.
- Buy fruit canned in fruit juice, not syrup.
- Instead of a sticky dessert, have a platter of fresh fruit slices with a couple of tablespoons of natural yoghurt or low-fat fromage frais. Or stir a mashed banana or a puréed mango into a natural yoghurt and sprinkle a tablespoon of chopped nuts on the top.
- Keep low-sugar snacks on hand for munchy moments – try a few unsalted nuts, a handful of seeds or some plain popcorn.
- If you must give in to your sweet tooth, have a couple of squares of good-quality chocolate (70 per cent cocoa solids or more) instead of a bar of chocolate candy.
- Drink water or diluted fresh fruit juice instead of squash, bought fruit-juice drinks and fizzy drinks. Some cans of drink contain as much as 13 teaspoons of sugar and 'diet' drinks are loaded with artificial sweeteners.

Beware of hidden sugars

Many breakfast cereals and tinned foods (such as beans and spaghetti) have high levels of sugar. And many foods promoted as 'low-fat' may have high sugar levels instead.

"Natural sugars in fruit come packaged with a whole variety of other nutrients, such as vitamins, minerals and fibre"

Types of sugar – not all are bad

Added sugar is often sucrose, which is quickly used and absorbed by the body, giving a blood-sugar boost that all too quickly fades.

But some fresh foods contain natural sugars. For example, fruit contains fructose, and milk contains lactose. The body absorbs these sugars less quickly, so they sustain us for longer. Another advantage of these natural sugars is that they also come packaged with a whole variety of other nutrients, such as protein, vitamins, minerals and fibre.

Artificial sweeteners

Scientists are still not 100 per cent sure of the safety of artificial sweeteners, particularly in children, and sweeteners also encourage children to develop a sweet tooth.

Many processed foods contain artificial sweeteners and so are best avoided where possible. You'll commonly find them in ice-lollies, yoghurts and desserts, ice cream, flavoured crisps, sauces, cakes, biscuits and ready meals. If you don't want to eat these chemicals, keep your eyes open for them on the labels. You'll find plenty of products without them. Examples of artificial sweeteners include aspartame, sorbitol, saccharine and acesulphame K.

Chapter Two
Cooking

HEALTHY COOKING

When healthy eating is your goal, *how* you cook is almost as important as *what* you cook. There's little point in buying a beautiful fillet of fresh fish and then covering it in a heavy batter and dunking it in a bath of boiling fat!

Concentrate your efforts on preparing your food as simply and as healthily as you can. Dump the deep fat fryer and oodles of oil and switch to steaming, baking, stir-frying, grilling, poaching and dry frying.

Stir-frying

Stir-frying is one of the healthiest cooking methods. Food is cooked for a short time, so it retains its nutrients, colour and flavour and very little oil is used.

- Have everything to hand before you start stir-frying. Chop all of the ingredients and mix together any sauces you are using.
- All of the ingredients should be cut into similar-sized pieces.
- Heat your wok before adding the oil.
- Use mild-flavoured oils that can withstand high heat, such as corn or groundnut oil (in moderation).
- If you are using meat in the dish, cook this and remove from the pan before cooking any vegetables. Return the meat to the pan to heat through just before serving.
- Add harder vegetables such as onion, carrot, baby corn and broccoli to the wok or pan first, adding soft vegetables that need a shorter cooking time (such as mushrooms, peppers, bean sprouts and greens) later.
- Add cooked noodles, herbs, sauces and nuts to the wok or pan just before the dish has finished cooking.

Basic stir-fry sauce

This basic sauce can be adapted to make a variety of tasty stir-fry dishes.

3 tbsp soy sauce
1 tbsp cornflour
3 tbsp dry sherry or Chinese rice wine
Pinch Chinese 5-spice powder (optional)
Ground black pepper

Mix the ingredients for the sauce together and set aside.

Prepare vegetables and meat or fish and stir-fry. Add the sauce, allow to thicken, and drizzle over a tablespoon of sesame oil.

Chicken-and-pepper stir-fry

(serves 4)

1. Prepare the basic stir-fry sauce.
2. Thinly slice three chicken breasts, 2 red peppers, 1 small chilli, 6 spring onions, a clove of garlic, and 8 small mushrooms.
3. Grate a 1-inch piece of fresh ginger, and wash 2 large handfuls of baby spinach leaves. Add a tablespoon of oil to a hot wok and stir-fry the ginger and garlic for 30 seconds.
4. Stir-fry the chicken until it is cooked and remove from the pan.
5. Stir-fry the other vegetables, adding the spinach and the sauce when the vegetables are cooked. Return the chicken to the pan and stir over the heat until the chicken is hot, the spinach wilted and the sauce has thickened. Drizzle over 1 teaspoon of sesame oil.

Simple hot and spicy prawn-and-tomato stir-fry

(serves 4)

1. Drain a can of Chinese water chestnuts and slice each chestnut into 4 even slices. Slice 2 tomatoes into thin wedges and slice one large clove of garlic. Grate a 1-inch piece of fresh ginger, slice a large carrot into very thin oblique slices and 6 spring onions into 1-inch slices. Defrost and rinse 450g of cooked, peeled prawns.

2. Make one batch of basic stir-fry sauce omitting the ground black pepper. Add to the sauce 2 tablespoons of tomato purée and $1/2$ teaspoon crushed Szechwan peppercorns.

3. Place 1 tablespoon of oil into a wok and add the peppercorns, garlic, and ginger. Fry for 30 seconds, then add the tomato wedges, carrot slices, water chestnuts and spring onions. Stir-fry for 2 minutes. Add the sauce and heat until thickened.

4. Add the cooked prawns and heat through (do not overcook the prawns, or they will be tough). Serve with some steamed broccoli and rice.

Roasting and baking

Tender cuts of meat, poultry and fish are all suited to the dry heat of oven cooking, and vegetables can be roasted, too. Remove excess fat from meat, and skin from poultry, before roasting on a rack in a non-stick roaster, so that any fat can drain away from the meat. Fish, vegetables and skinned boneless chicken breasts can also be baked in greaseproof-paper parcels.

> ### Handy tip
> A joint of meat will continue to cook for 5–10 minutes after it is removed from the oven.

Lamb chops with crumb-and-mint crust

(serves 4)

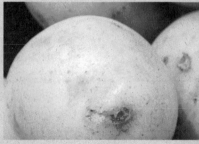

1. Heat the oven to 190°C/Gas 5.
2. Take 4 lamb steaks (fat removed) and place on a baking sheet. Season with freshly ground black pepper.
3. Combine 50g/2oz fresh wholemeal breadcrumbs with 2 tablespoons wholemeal jelly and spoon on to the top of the lamb steaks.
4. Bake in the oven for 20–30 minutes depending on the thickness of the meat. Serve with boiled new potatoes, broccoli and sweetcorn.

"Tender cuts of meat, poultry and fish are all suited to the dry heat of oven cooking, and vegetables can be roasted, too"

Mustard and honey chicken
(serves 4)

1. Preheat the oven to 190°C/Gas 5.
2. Place 4 skinless chicken breasts into a roasting pan. Combine 4 tablespoons wholegrain mustard with 2 tablespoons runny honey and spoon over the chicken breasts.

3. Bake for 25 minutes or until the chicken is cooked through. Baste the chicken with the pan juices during cooking.
4. Serve with a baked jacket potato and large green salad.

Baked cod with Mediterranean topping
(serves 4)

1. Preheat the oven to 180°C/Gas 4.
2. Take 4 white fish fillets (such as cod, haddock, coley) and lay in an ovenproof dish.

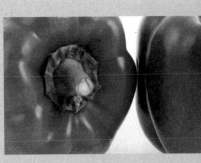

3. Finely chop 1 small red pepper, 1 small green pepper, one small onion, 1 garlic clove, 4 medium mushrooms. Combine in a bowl with a teaspoon of olive oil. Spoon the topping on to the fillets and bake in the oven for 20 minutes or until the fish is cooked through.
4. Serve with new potatoes and fresh vegetables or a salad.

Poaching

Poaching in water or stock is a healthy cooking method – and no fat is needed. It's useful for cooking vegetables, chicken, fish and eggs.

Stewing and casseroling

Stewing and casseroling are good methods to use when you are cooking less tender cuts of meat. Always remove visible fat from the meat and use a heavy-based saucepan to prevent the food from sticking to the bottom if you're cooking on top of the stove, rather than in the oven. Cook on a slow heat and stir occasionally. Vegetables and pulses (beans and lentils) can also be made into stews.

Tomato and mixed-bean stew

(serves 4)

1. Chop a large onion and place in a saucepan with 2 cloves of garlic, crushed, and a finely chopped small red chilli. Sauté in a teaspoon of oil for 3 minutes.
2. Add a large can of chopped tomatoes, 8 tablespoons of water, freshly ground black pepper and 2 tins of mixed beans, rinsed and drained. Simmer gently for 10 minutes adding a little more water if necessary.
3. Just before serving, add a handful of chopped flat-leaf parsley or coriander and a tablespoon of natural yoghurt. Serve with brown rice.

Steaming

No oil is needed when food is steamed. It is an excellent way to retain the vitamins and minerals when cooking vegetables. When you boil vegetables you lose a lot of the water-soluble vitamins (the B vitamins and vitamin C) into the cooking water.

Grilling

Grilling is another healthy cooking option, since fat can run off and only the smallest amount of oil is needed to prevent the food from drying out. Marinades can also be used to help keep grilled food moist.

Handy tip

You'll use much less oil for roasting, frying and grilling if you brush or lightly spray the food with oil, rather than the whole pan.

Flavour boosters

- Fry three sticks of finely chopped celery and a handful of chopped walnuts in a teaspoon of olive oil for three minutes. Sprinkle over stews just before serving for added crunch.
- Add a few sprigs of rosemary and a few garlic cloves to potatoes when you roast them.
- A tablespoon of prune juice adds flavour to stews and casseroles.
- Squeeze the juice of half an orange into the water when boiling carrots.
- Finely chop a couple of anchovies and add them to a potato salad.
- Halve a lemon and slip it into a whole chicken before roasting for a delicate citrus flavour.

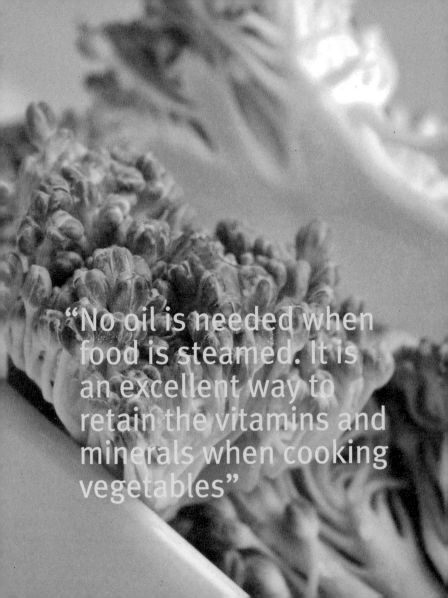

"No oil is needed when food is steamed. It is an excellent way to retain the vitamins and minerals when cooking vegetables"

- Grate a little nutmeg over spinach before serving.
- Add a hint of ginger to pan-fried chicken or salmon by adding a few slices of fresh ginger to the pan with the oil and cooking for two minutes. Remove before adding the salmon or chicken.
- Sprinkle a tablespoon of toasted pumpkin, sunflower or sesame seeds over cooked broccoli or Brussels sprouts to add crunch.

Five twenty-minute feasts

- A mushroom omelette, with two small jacket potatoes (cooked in the microwave) and grilled tomato halves.
- Veggie or chicken stir-fry with plenty of vegetables, served with whole-wheat noodles.
- Wholemeal pasta, with a sauce made from tinned tomatoes cooked with finely chopped onion and fresh or dried herbs, with a tin of tuna for protein. Throw in some olives if you like.
- A piece of fish baked in the oven, with a herb and crumb topping, served with new potatoes and fresh vegetables.
- A tin of salmon served with a large salad and boiled new potatoes.

Handy tip

Beware of supermarket 'ready meals', since many are high in unhealthy fat, calories and salt. Even the 'healthy' ranges are often less than virtuous – so always check the labels carefully, or, better still, make your own and pop them in the freezer to use when time is short.

CALMER COOKING

Make your time in the kitchen relaxed by planning a week's evening meals and doing some advance preparation. Choose simple, quick-to-prepare evening meals and leave your *cordon bleu* efforts for the weekends and when you have more time. Twenty minutes to half an hour is all that is needed to cook a nutritious meal.

Get some kitchen calm

- Keep your kitchen tidy, and your work surfaces clear. It's quicker and easier to work in a clear area.
- Make a note of any days in the coming week that are going to be particularly busy or stressful. Then plan especially quick and easy meals for those days.
- Check out the fresh-fish counter for white fish, and oily fish such as salmon, sardines and mackerel. They are delicious simply grilled with a large salad and boiled new potatoes. Fresh fish takes so little time to prepare.
- Make the most of labour-saving devices such as food processors, smoothie makers and electric health grills.

Make your freezer work for you

Getting organised is the key to using your freezer efficiently. Keep your freezer well stocked and you will be able to knock up a healthy meal in no time at all.

- Make meal-sized portions of your favourite basic tomato-based sauces for pasta. When you reheat them you can simply add beans, mushrooms, asparagus, courgettes, broccoli, olives or feta cheese.

- When you make a soup, stew, casserole or Bolognese sauce, make a double quantity and freeze half to use later.

- Freeze meal-sized portions of your favourite homemade curry sauce so that you can quickly make a chicken, fish or vegetable curry to serve with brown rice.

- Freeze whole sprigs of robust herbs such as rosemary, parsley, mint and sage in small bags to add to a soup, casserole or stew. All you have to do is take out what you need and crumble it straight into the saucepan.

- Make the most of summer berries by freezing them loose on trays, then packing them into bags. Then you will have raspberries, blackberries and blueberries to add to winter breakfast cereal and yoghurts and to make delicious desserts.

- If you've got a glut of oranges in the fruit bowl, freeze the juice in paper cups. If you take them out of the freezer before you go to bed and put them in the fridge, you'll have a refreshing glass of juice for breakfast.

- Stew fruit for ready-made pie fillings. Stew the fruit, place into ovenproof pie dishes and freeze. When it has frozen, remove the filling from the dish and put the filling back into the freezer. Then, when you want to make a quick pudding, all you have to do is pop the fruit back into the dish, defrost it, and add a pastry, sponge or crumble topping.
- Keep a loaf of sliced wholemeal bread in the freezer in case you run out of toast for breakfast. Most modern toasters have a setting for frozen bread.
- Keep a bag of frozen prawns in the freezer to make quick stir-fries, salads, curries and sandwiches.
- Make batches of veggie burgers, bean burgers, turkey burgers and chicken burgers – so you'll have your own healthy fast food on hand.

GET THE GADGETS

You don't need a kitchen full of electronic wizardry and the latest gadgets, but a few carefully chosen items can make life easier. Here are a few that it's worthwhile investing in.

- A few good-quality knives and saucepans. This is a personal thing, but get the best you can afford – choose the ones you like the feel of. If you don't like them, you won't use them!
- An electric health grill or ridged griddle pan – these allow fat to drain away when you're cooking meat. They're also good for cooking fish and chicken breasts.

- An electric 'stick blender' – great for avoiding lumps in sauces, and puréeing soups while they're still in the saucepan!
- A liquidiser – just the thing for creating thick warming soups and making purées of fruit or vegetables.
- A steamer – an electric steamer or a steamer basket for fitting inside a saucepan will ensure that your vegetables retain as much of their nutrients as possible. If you boil them, a lot of the goodness gets thrown away with the water.

Toasted-sandwich ideas

- Spread a slice of wholemeal bread with mango chutney. Add ham and a little crumbled mature cheddar. Put a second slice of bread on top and grill or cook in a sandwich press.
- Spread a slice of wholemeal bread with horseradish sauce. Add some sliced, lean, cold beef and sliced gherkins. Add the second slice and grill or cook in a sandwich press.
- Spread a slice of wholemeal bread with tomato purée. Drain a tin of sardines in oil and mash the fish. Pile on top of the tomato purée. Add a few slices of tomato. Add the second slice of bread and grill or cook in a sandwich press.
- Spread a slice of wholemeal bread with low-fat cream cheese. Add a sliced banana and a drizzle of honey. Top with the second slice and grill or cook in a sandwich press.
- Spread a slice of wholemeal bread with a little cranberry sauce. Add some slices of cold cooked turkey and season with freshly ground pepper. Top with the second slice and grill or cook in a sandwich press.

"A liquidiser is perfect for making thick soups or for puréeing fruit and vegetables"

Chapter Three
Eating on the move

HEALTHY EATING AWAY FROM HOME

When you're out and about – travelling, away on business, or having a shopping day – it's all too easy to let your good eating habits fly out of the window. Regular mealtimes can fall by the wayside, and you may have to rely on someone else to do the cooking and to choose the ingredients.

But, with a little nutritional know-how and forward planning, you can eat healthily, wherever you are.

Handy tip

Start the day with a sustaining wholegrain breakfast such as low-sugar cereal with yoghurt, or porridge made with skimmed milk. The grains provide slow-release energy, and the protein in the milk or yoghurt helps sustain you for longer. Add some vitamin-rich fresh fruit – berries, chopped apple or a sliced banana.

PICNICS AND PACKED LUNCHES

Whether you're working away from home, planning a day out, travelling by train or facing a long wait at an airport, taking a packed lunch rather than dashing in to a pub or fast-food restaurant keeps you in charge of the menu – and saves money, too. Likewise, if your job involves lots of travelling, you won't need to rely on greasy-spoon cafés and motorway service stations if you bring your own lunch.

If you decide to take a packed lunch and know you'll be eating in the car or on a park bench, don't choose runny fillings. Consider making a wholemeal pitta pocket or a fajita wrap as an alternative to a sandwich. Then all you need to complete a nutritious lunch is a piece of fruit and some bottled water (mineral water, or a bottle refilled from the tap) to stop you becoming dehydrated. If you don't think that's filling enough, add a low-fat natural yoghurt, or, as an occasional treat, a healthy homemade bar (see the recipe on Page 58) or cake. Remember to keep your lunch in a cool bag with an ice block.

Here are some on-the-go sandwich ideas (they're equally good in a roll, pitta or wrap):

- sliced roast chicken, with crispy lettuce and pepper strips
- tinned tuna with lettuce and finely chopped cucumber
- low-fat grated cheese with apple slices and lettuce
- well-drained cottage cheese, grated carrot and grated apple
- low-fat cream cheese, tomato, cucumber and lettuce
- low-fat soft cheese, lean ham and sliced tomato
- sliced hardboiled egg with lettuce and tomato slices
- peanut butter with sliced cucumber
- sliced vegetarian sausage with pickle and lettuce
- cooked sliced chicken with salad vegetables and pickle

Shop-bought sandwiches – a word of caution

Some bought sandwiches can tot up a colossal 750 calories, and a hefty serving of fat, so look for healthy and reduced-calorie options. Check the label for calories, salt and fat (especially saturated fat).

- Skip any containing mayonnaise or creamy dressings or large amounts of hard cheese, since these are high in saturated fat.
- Opt for sandwiches containing some protein – fish, lean meat, poultry or low-fat cheese – with plenty of salad and (if necessary) a low-fat dressing.
- If you are lucky enough to find a sandwich bar that makes sandwiches to order, you'll be able to devise your own healthy sandwich – but take care. Fillings are often very generous and it's easy to pile in the calories.

Snack attacks

Try to keep to regular mealtimes if you can when you are out and about, but keep a few healthy energy-boosting snacks handy for times when this isn't possible. Healthy snacks include:

- fruit (bananas, apples, pears, oranges, or a pot of washed strawberries or grapes, are all easy to eat)
- a bag of dried fruit (sultanas, raisins, dried apple rings, dried apricots).
- plain popcorn (not toffee or salted); you can add a sprinkling of pepper or chilli to liven it up
- a currant bun
- a scone (preferably wholemeal, spread with a little low-sugar jam if you like)

- oatcakes lightly spread with low-fat cream cheese and sandwiched together
- vegetable strips (try sweet pepper, carrots, cucumber and celery)
- small bags of unsalted nuts and seeds (try peanuts, brazils, almonds, sunflower and pumpkin seeds)
- homemade bagel crisps (see the recipe on Page 59)
- homemade energy bars (see the recipe below)

Energy bar

This nutty, fruity bar provides slow-release energy.

75g low-fat spread
3 tbsp set honey
2 tbsp water
150g porridge oats
½ tsp cinnamon
50g walnuts, roughly chopped
25g pumpkin seeds
25g sunflower seeds
25g desiccated coconut
75g raisins or sultanas
5 ready-to-eat dried apricots, roughly chopped
3 dates, roughly chopped
10g sesame seeds

1. Preheat the oven.
2. Melt the low-fat spread, honey and water in a large saucepan over a low heat. Cook for three or four minutes, stirring continuously, until it resembles a thick sauce.
3. Add all the remaining ingredients and stir to mix thoroughly.
4. Line a 30 x 19cm Swiss roll tin with nonstick baking parchment.
5. Spoon the mixture into the tin and flatten the surface.
6. Bake for 25–30 minutes until the mixture is firm to the touch and a light golden colour.
7. Remove from the oven, loosen the edges with a knife and leave to cool for 10 minutes.
8. Mark the bar into small squares and cut. Store in an airtight tin.

Bagel crisps

When you want a low-fat alternative to shop-bought crisps, try making your own bagel crisps. They're delicious and easy to make.

Simply slice bagels horizontally into thin rounds. Lightly brush the surfaces with olive oil (you can flavour it with a little garlic or chilli paste) and then bake in a slow oven (150°C/Gas 2) until they are lightly toasted and crisp. Keep an eye on them so they don't burn. They'll keep in an airtight container for a few days without losing their crispness.

EATING OUT AND ABOUT

It *is* possible to make healthy choices when you're eating out and about. Even burger restaurants have some healthier options – if you know what to look for.

Coffee bars

It's the milk and sugar in your coffee that bumps up the fat and calorie count, so go for these low-fat options.

An Americano taken black with no sugar has zero calories. Cappuccinos are lower than lattes (less milk), and you can save fat and calories by having 'skinny' (skimmed-milk) versions. While a medium-skinny latte weighs in at about 160 calories, having full-fat milk bumps the total up to around 270, and a shot of flavoured syrup adds another 15 or so calories.

And, if you're sensitive to caffeine's stimulant effects, go for a decaff. Probably the healthiest drinks options are tea (many outlets now also serve herbal versions), fruit juice, fresh fruit smoothies and – best of all – mineral water.

If you need something to eat, skip the muffins – even those sold as 'skinny' or 'low-fat' can be 400 calories and regular muffins can stack up an amazing 600 calories. Opt for a scone or a biscotti instead.

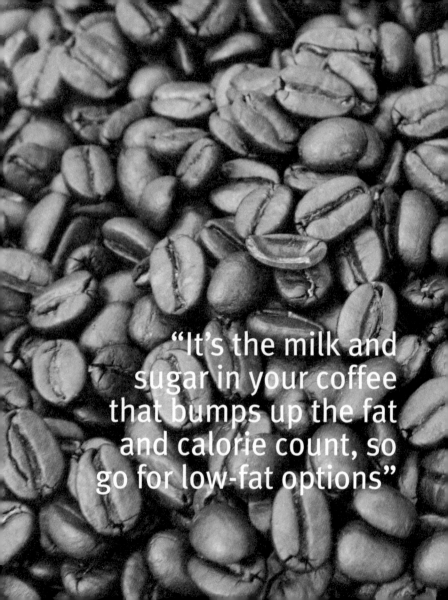

"It's the milk and sugar in your coffee that bumps up the fat and calorie count, so go for low-fat options"

Department store and supermarket cafés

These are improving and if you choose carefully you can get a healthy meal or snack. Choose from these:

- a crisp salad with lean meat, fish or cottage cheese
- soup and a crusty roll
- a 'healthy option' prepacked sandwich, wrap or ciabatta
- a baked potato with cottage cheese or baked beans (steer clear of prawns and mayo, grated cheese and coleslaw)
- a scone with low-fat spread
- a rock cake
- a currant bun or slice of fruit loaf

Avoid:

- lasagne
- curry
- fish and chips
- sausage and chips
- fresh cream cakes
- apple pie
- ice cream
- cheesecake

Don't be tempted by the all-day-breakfast. Unless, that is, you give the bacon, fried bread, hash browns, sausages, black pudding and fried eggs a miss and settle for a more healthy baked tomato, mushrooms, baked beans and scrambled egg. If you take a nine- or eleven-item special breakfast, you could end up with a plate containing more than 1,100 calories – and that's without the toast, butter and marmalade!

Pizza places
Choose from:
- a thin and crispy pizza rather than a deep-pan or cheese-stuffed-crust pizza
- tuna, prawns, pineapple and vegetables as toppings, and ask the waiter if you can go easy on the cheese
- a main-meal salad (avoiding items with creamy and oily dressings); have a side helping of potato wedges, to fill you up, if you must – they're fried, but do contain some fibre in the skins

Avoid:
- stuffed crust pizza
- meat or sausage fillings
- lashings of cheese
- fried onion rings – they really are fat traps
- garlic bread
- lasagne or pasta in creamy sauce – they're packed with saturated fat

Burger bars and other fast food chains
Many burger restaurants are smartening up their act, with low-fat options available.

Choose from:
- a chicken or fish grill
- a salad (watch out for high-fat dressings)
- fresh fruit
- vegetable sticks
- fresh fruit juice

Avoid:

- burgers
- battered chicken
- French fries
- high-fat creamy dressings
- ice cream, doughnuts, muffins
- thick shakes

A drinks minefield

Some of the large fizzy drinks sold in fast-food chains can contain nearly 250 calories and 11 teaspoons of sugar. And 'thick shakes' can pack more than 500 calories, 13g of fat and 16 teaspoons of sugar. That's 17 per cent of your fat and over one and a half times your recommended daily sugar allowance slipping down so easily. Diet drinks are low-calorie, but think about whether you want all those chemical sweeteners. Mineral water is the healthiest option of all, but, if you don't fancy that, go for fruit juice, tea or coffee (if the caffeine doesn't make you jittery).

Many of the fast-food chains have leaflets available showing the calories, fat and sugar in their meals. Make a point of reading these, to avoid any nutritional nasties.

Fish-and-chip shops

Admittedly fish-and-chip shops are one of the hardest places to eat healthy. Save them for very occasional treats only!

- Order fish, but eat only the fish – leave the batter.
- If you must, have just a small portion of chips. Thick chips are marginally better than thin chips, since they have less surface area and so absorb less fat when they're fried.

Pubs

It is not always easy to find a simple healthy lunch in a pub. Often, pub grub is delivered on huge platters with servings to match. If healthy choices are few and far between on the menu, settle for the old favourite of a chicken-and-salad sandwich or a baked potato with a low-fat filling. Choose from:

- grilled meat or chicken with salad
- grilled salmon or white fish
- jacket potatoes with a low-fat filling, such as tuna, salmon, baked beans or cottage cheese.
- wholemeal sandwiches with ham or chicken filling, and salad

Avoid:

- creamy lasagne and macaroni cheese
- anything fried
- anything with pastry
- anything served with mayonnaise
- pâté

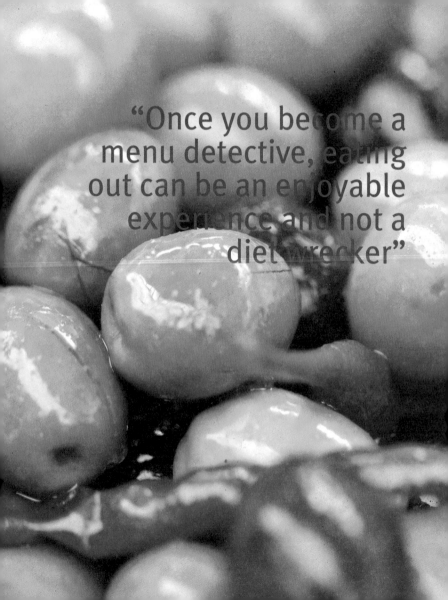

"Once you become a menu detective, eating out can be an enjoyable experience and not a diet wrecker"

TREAT YOURSELF: DINING OUT IN RESTAURANTS

Once you become a menu detective, eating out can be an enjoyable experience and not a diet wrecker. Work out what is likely to be in a dish and how it has been cooked. If you're not sure whether something has been fried or whether a sauce contains oodles of cream, ask the waiter.

Get to know which dishes are likely to be high in fat or sugar. Look for restaurants where food is cooked to order – even if you have to wait a little longer for your meal to arrive. Steer clear of choices described as 'crispy' or 'crunchy' – the chances are they will have been deep-fried. Other words to be wary of are 'breaded', 'smothered' and, more obviously, 'fried'.

Top tips for eating out

- Choose grilled, baked, poached or steamed breast of chicken or fish, because they will be lower in fat.
- Don't be tempted by the savoury nibbles that may be offered while you are waiting for your meal to arrive.
- Don't assume that a vegetarian option will be lower in fat – always check. They may include cheesy sauces that are full of fat.
- Select dishes cooked in tomato-based sauces instead of cream and cheese sauces.
- If a dish includes a sauce or gravy, ask to have it served separately so that you can add as little as you need.
- Check whether vegetables are served with butter. If they are, ask for yours to come without – you can save a lot of calories this way.
- Ask to have your salad served without dressing, or with the dressing served separately.

- Order a starter as your main course and ask for it to be served with a large salad or plain boiled or steamed vegetables.
- Select a starter or a dessert that you can share. That way you can still have a treat, but a smaller portion of it.
- Skip chips and roast potatoes and choose rice or a jacket potato to accompany your meal.
- Choose a fresh fruit salad or a sorbet for dessert – both are packed full of vitamins and are fat-free.
- Don't be tempted to order more food than you need. If you notice that portions being served to diners on other tables are larger than you would like, ask for a smaller portion when you order.
- If side salads appear small, ask for a larger one or a 'double' order.
- Try to avoid or limit alcohol – on top of the hefty number of calories it can contain, alcohol can make you relax and you can then easily lose sight of your healthy eating habits.
- Eat slowly – it'll give your brain a chance to get the 'I'm full' message.

Quiz: questions of health

If you know your way round restaurant menus, it's simple to spot the high-fat and high-sugar traps.

Can you identify the healthier options from this menu? You'll find two in each course.

Starters

- ○ grilled spicy king prawns
- ○ cannelloni-and-tomato salad
- ○ toasted goat's cheese with garlic croutons and salad leaves
- ○ chicken satay
- ○ minestrone soup
- ○ crispy fried duck with Chinese pancakes

Main courses

- ○ pasta carbonara with green salad and garlic bread
- ○ grilled chilli-glazed salmon, with watercress and new potatoes
- ○ bean-and-chorizo cassoulet with broccoli
- ○ pasta with a tomato, mushroom and olive sauce
- ○ three-cheese quiche with potato wedges and tomato salad
- ○ steak-and-kidney pudding with green beans and new potatoes

Desserts

- ○ ice-cream sundae with whipped-cream topping
- ○ apple pie and clotted cream
- ○ raspberry sorbet with warm mango purée
- ○ tiramisu trifle
- ○ baked apple with Greek yoghurt
- ○ Black Forest gateaux

Answers to quiz: starters: grilled spicy king prawns; minestrone soup; main course: grilled chilli glazed salmon with watercress and new potatoes; pasta with a tomato, mushroom and olive sauce; dessert: raspberry sorbet with warm mango purée; baked apple with Greek yoghurt

FOREIGN FARE AND TAKEAWAYS

There is no denying it: takeaway food is popular. But it's a sad fact that much of it is staggeringly high in saturated fat and salt, and low in fibre, vitamins and minerals.

When you send out for the occasional takeaway, here's how to make the more healthy choices. Many of the less healthy dishes you find on takeaway menus often also appear on restaurant menus, so be warned.

Indian

Smart choices

- Dishes cooked in the tandoor (an oven for cooking food quickly at high temperature) are the lowest-fat options you'll find. Go for tandoori chicken or tandoori king prawns, or chicken or lamb tikka, served with salad. You could opt for a starter-sized portion of a tandoori or tikka dish with a double-sized salad. (Beware the tikka masala dishes: they come with a sauce that is high in fat.)
- Curries with tomato-based sauces.
- Dhal – a lentil-based vegetable dish.
- Plain boiled rice.
- Chapattis.
- Raita – an accompaniment made with yoghurt and cucumber.

To be avoided

- Fried poppadoms.
- Dishes with cream (tikka masala, korma, pasanda). Avoid any dishes described as 'creamy' or 'rich'.
- Anything deep-fried or high in fat, such as bhajis, samosa, pakora, pilau rice, naan bread, poppadoms. Naan breads are real fat traps, and fruity Peshawari naan has lots of added sugar, fruit and coconut.
- Biryani – this mixture of rice, meat, vegetables, fruit and nuts can by high in fat and sugar.
- Chutneys – these are often high in sugar or oil.

An Indian buffet may give you an opportunity to taste a wonderful array of dishes, but choose carefully, or you can easily overload on fat and sugar.

Chinese

Smart choices
- Stir-fried vegetable dishes (with or without bean curd, chicken or prawns).
- Steamed dim sums.
- Grilled fish dishes.
- Hot and sour dishes.
- Tofu dishes.
- Boiled rice and boiled noodles.
- Dishes described as 'baked' or 'steamed'.

To be avoided

- Anything deep-fried or battered, such as prawn toasts, crispy noodles, spring rolls and prawn crackers.
- Duck dishes, meat with visible fat and poultry with skin on.
- Sticky spare ribs and sweet-and-sour dishes.
- Pork balls – they will be battered and deep-fried.
- Fried rice dishes.
- Any dish described as 'sizzling', or 'crispy', as it will probably have been fried.

Thai

Smart choices

- Steamed dim sum.
- Stir-fried or steamed vegetable, chicken, prawn or bean-curd dishes.
- Plain boiled or steamed rice.
- Grilled or steamed fish dishes.
- Hot and sour soups.

To be avoided

- Red, green and yellow curries, and any coconut-cream-based dishes.
- Duck dishes.
- Anything deep-fried (such as spring rolls and prawn toasts).
- Spare ribs and sweet-and-sour dishes.
- Sticky rice, fried rice or fried noodles.
- Satay – it's usually served with a high-fat peanut sauce.

Italian

The traditional Mediterranean diet has plenty to recommend it, thanks to its reliance on plenty of fresh vegetables and heart-healthy olive oil. But, sadly, the 'Italian' food we eat in the UK is often a far cry from this healthy ideal.

Smart choices

- Thin and crispy pizzas.
- Pizza toppings of mushrooms, peppers, onions, sweetcorn, chicken, prawns, ham, tuna. Ask for less cheese.
- Pasta with tomato-based sauces.
- Grilled fish.
- Vegetable soups.

To be avoided

- Deep-pan and stuffed-crust pizzas.
- Toppings that include salami, pepperoni, other processed meats or extra cheese.
- Creamy pasta dishes such as carbonara and lasagne.
- Garlic bread. This can pile on the calories, so, if you really can't resist, make sure it is something you share.
- Platters of antipasto – they're often heavy on the meat and cheese. If you decide to have one as a starter, make it a dish that you share.
- Bruschetta – it's often brushed with oil before and during cooking and can be surprisingly high in fat. Focaccia can also be high in fat.
- If you see the words 'Fritto misto' on the menu give it a miss – it's a mixture of battered and deep-fried vegetables, meat and seafood.
- Spicy Italian sausages – they are often very fatty.

Watch the pasta serving sizes. Pasta is an inexpensive ingredient and you will often find servings many times larger than the 50g/2oz recommended on the packets you use at home.

Risottos can also be a calorie minefield, so always ask whether the dish contains cream or butter. The delicious creamy taste of risotto should come from the rice itself, but to save time many restaurants add cream or butter. Opt for seafood- or tomato-based risottos, because these are less likely to be loaded with fat.

Spanish

Spanish food can be very healthy, but you need to know what to look for, since there are also dishes drenched in oil. It's likely to be healthy olive oil, but it's still high in calories.

Tapas bars are becoming more popular and are an ideal way to get a feel for Spanish cuisine, provided you choose wisely. Ask your waiter how the dishes are prepared and avoid any that are less than healthy.

Smart choices

- Vegetable-based soups.
- Tomato and seafood dishes.
- Grilled fish.

To be avoided

- Sausages such as chorizo.
- Food that is breaded and deep-fried.

At home with the takeaway taste

If you enjoy the takeaway taste, why not create your own healthy version at home? It's simple and not expensive.

Burgers

Make your own burgers using lean beef, lamb or chicken, with onions and seasonings, and grill them slowly. Serve with a crunchy salad and tasty relishes and salsas.

Fish and chips

Instead of battered fish, buy fillets of fish from your fishmonger or supermarket and make your own crispy crumbed fish. Cut the fillets into 2.5cm/1-inch-wide strips. Dip the fish in lightly beaten egg white seasoned with mustard powder, garlic or fresh chopped herbs and then into dried wholemeal breadcrumbs or crushed cornflakes. Place on baking parchment, spray with a little oil, and bake in the oven until the fish is cooked and the coating crisp.

Oven chips

Take some large potatoes, peel them if you must, but preferably leave the skins on. Cut into thick chips and parboil for 3 minutes. Drain and pat dry with kitchen paper and place on baking parchment. Lightly spray the chips with oil. Bake in the oven at medium heat (200°C/Gas 6) for half an hour until they are brown and crispy. Turn several times while they are cooking. If they brown too quickly, reduce the oven heat. Serve your fish and chips with grilled tomatoes and peas or a colourful salad.

Pizza

Make or buy a pizza base and construct your own topping. Put a small tin of chopped tomatoes into a saucepan with a half-teaspoon of dried mixed herbs and boil gently for about 10 minutes until much of the liquid has evaporated and you have a thick paste. Spread the cooled paste over the pizza base. Then add one of these tasty toppings

- Arrange sliced tomatoes, mushrooms and thinly sliced onion rings on top. Sprinkle over some sweetcorn, and a very small amount of grated cheese. Season with black pepper, and add some basil leaves if you like.

- Arrange some thinly sliced mushrooms over the pizza and add some chopped lean ham, a couple of chopped pineapple rings, some sweetcorn and a little grated cheese.

- Top the pizza with sliced tomato, strips of red and green pepper, a handful of roughly torn basil leaves, if you like, and sprinkle over a little grated cheese.

- Arrange sliced tomato, strips of green pepper, and sliced mushroom over the pizza base and top with drained sardines arranged like the spokes of a wheel.

- Add flaked tuna, flaked salmon or strips of cooked chicken to a pizza topped with sliced tomatoes and mushrooms.

The secret of a healthy pizza is to go easy on the cheese and other high-fat toppings. Try using ricotta, which is naturally lower in fat than many cheeses, and, if you need extra taste, sprinkle a little strongly flavoured parmesan on the pizza when it comes out of the oven.

Bake your pizza in the centre of the oven (180°C/Gas 4) for 15–20 minutes until the base is crisp and the cheese is melted and golden.Serve with a large salad.

Homemade chicken nuggets

Cut skinned chicken breasts into 6–8 pieces. Dip the pieces of chicken into beaten egg and then in fine, dried wholemeal breadcrumbs. (For extra flavour, add a pinch of paprika to the breadcrumbs.) Place the coated chicken on a baking tray and spray lightly with oil. Bake the chicken in a preheated oven (180°C/Gas 4) for 20 minutes or until the chicken is cooked through.

Serve with homemade oven chips and a large salad.

ON HOLIDAY

It's easy to stray from healthy good intentions when you're on holiday. But so long as you make sensible choices – at least most of the time – you can have a great holiday without undoing all the good you have done at home.

● Every country has its healthy options – it's just a matter of finding them. And one of the wonderful things about many foreign holiday destinations is that you'll often discover local food stalls and markets in even the smallest towns and villages selling fantastic fruit – the perfect any-time snack – and restaurants serving fish straight from the sea and delicious fresh local produce. Could there be anything nicer than eating melons that were on the plant a few hours earlier or grilled fish cooked at a beachside restaurant, as you sip a long cool glass of freshly pressed fruit juice?

- Make the most of the opportunity to try new dishes, and sample exotic fruit and vegetables. Who knows? You might come back from your trip with some new recipes and a jar or two of a local speciality to spice up your cooking at home.
- Even if you are not very adventurous when it comes to food, 'international cuisine' of the kind you're used to is available in most countries. Whatever you do, don't be tempted to slip into a pizza, chips and burger habit when you are on holiday!
- When you are eating out abroad, follow the same rules as you would if you were eating in a restaurant at home, and consider the fat, sugar and salt that are likely to be in any dish you choose.

Self-catering

Many of us opt for a self-catering holiday at some time. The secret of self-catering holidays is to keep meals simple, so that you don't feel you are simply exchanging a kitchen you know for one that you don't. There is no reason to be stuck in the kitchen while everyone else is enjoying themselves.

Get prepared before you go. If you are travelling to your holiday destination by car, it's easy to take enough food for the first couple of meals so you don't have to shop the moment you arrive. Before you go shopping try to make a list of things you'll need – it'll save you valuable time and money.

- Make the most of markets and shops where you can buy locally grown produce and fresh meat, fish and poultry. Look and see where the locals do their shopping.
- Decant a little of your favourite herbs and spices into tiny plastic bags or pots before you go, to add flavour to simple dishes.
- Keep meals simple – such as grilled fish or chicken, a jacket potato and a salad, followed by some fresh fruit; or a quick bean chilli with a salad and crusty bread followed by a yoghurt and fruit.
- Enlist the help of the family in preparing meals.
- Take advantage of the weather and eat meals outside in the shade when you can.
- If you're holidaying overseas, always follow the food-safety advice regarding whether it is safe to drink tap water, to have ice in drinks or eat salads and so on.
- If there is a safe and suitable site, have a barbecue – a piece of marinated meat, chicken or fish with a salad and some chunks of crusty wholemeal bread makes the perfect al fresco meal for all the family. Or try some fresh-vegetable kebabs with a yoghurt-and-herb dipping sauce, a large salad and some fruit.

Chapter Four
Healthy lunches for grown-ups and kids

you are™
what
you eat.

PACKED LUNCHES FOR ADULTS

Preparing a packed lunch for yourself or your family does not have to be boring or time-consuming. Use some imagination to make it a healthy feast.

Try not to skip lunch. A nutritious meal provides you with the energy to sail through the afternoon, without the temptation to reach for a packet of crisps or a chocolate bar to keep you going until suppertime. Here are three tips for healthy lunching.

- Try to get away from your desk and relax while you eat your lunch.
- Combine lunch with a walk in the park or some window shopping.
- If you have a workplace canteen, check out the healthy options. If there aren't any, raise it with the management.

Taking your own packed lunch to work will:
- save you money
- give you control over what you eat
- help you keep your diet packed with vital nutrients

What is a healthy packed lunch?

Lunch (wherever you eat it and whether or not you make it yourself) should provide both adults and children with approximately one third of their daily energy requirements as well as a third of their protein, carbohydrate, fibre, vitamins and minerals. It also shouldn't 'overshoot' one-third of their recommended maximums for fat (especially saturated fat), sugar and salt.

Of course, there's no point in getting obsessive about the 'one-third' rule – if you compensate for a not-so-good lunch by eating 'better' for the rest of the day, it won't do you any harm.

For a healthy packed lunch, try to include:
- one portion of protein (meat, chicken, fish, eggs or a vegetarian alternative)
- one portion of a starchy carbohydrate food (wholemeal bread, wholemeal pasta, brown rice, wholewheat noodles)
- at least one portion of salad or vegetables
- one portion of low-fat dairy or calcium-rich food (yoghurt, milk, low-fat cheese)
- at least one portion of fruit (preferably fresh, or alternatively a small quantity of dried fruit or tinned fruit in juice)
- water and/or pure fruit juice (diluted for children)

Be adventurous when you're planning packed lunches. It's one meal for which you don't have to take the likes and dislikes of other members of the family into account.

The variety of sandwiches, wraps and meal salads you can make are almost endless, and you can always make use of leftovers from last night's dinner – or cook a little extra so there is something to save for your lunch. Here are a few non-sandwich lunch ideas based around leftovers:

"Be adventurous when planning packed lunches"

- cold homemade chicken curry and rice on a bed of salad vegetables
- a portion of rice and some cold stir-fried chicken and vegetables
- a little cold chicken or vegetable curry with a little low-fat mayonnaise and some lettuce leaves (it also makes a quick filling for a fajita wrap or pitta bread)
- a grilled fillet of salmon (do an extra one at suppertime the day before) combined with some cold cooked pasta and salad
- a portion of cold macaroni cheese and salad

Always take your lunch to work in a cool bag with an ice pack, particularly when the weather is warm. Transfer it to a fridge when you arrive, if you have one available.

Keep lunch exciting
To keep your lunch interesting, ring the changes by experimenting with different fillings and kinds of bread – try to go for those made with wholegrains. Pittas, wholemeal chapattis and wholemeal wraps can add to the variety.

Lunchbox sandwich fillings
Try these tasty and nutritious ideas:
- spicy stir-fried chicken and crispy lettuce-and-pepper strips
- roasted Mediterranean vegetables and salad leaves
- sliced poached chicken breast, low-fat mayonnaise or natural yoghurt and finely chopped salad vegetables
- tomato, lettuce and mozzarella cheese

- salmon, chopped cucumber, low-fat mayonnaise or natural yoghurt and lettuce
- chopped hardboiled egg, cress and low-fat mayonnaise or natural yoghurt
- chopped chicken, tossed in a little low-fat fromage frais, with salad
- turkey and low-fat coleslaw
- grated reduced-fat cheese with apple slices
- drained cottage cheese, grated carrot and grated apple
- tinned tuna, sweetcorn and pepper
- thinly sliced ham with grated carrot and salad
- thinly sliced roast beef with horseradish sauce and sliced tomato

Lunchbox salads
Lunchbox salads are light and refreshing and also full of essential vitamins or minerals.

Here are some protein-rich salad ideas:
- lettuce, sliced tomato, cucumber and spring onion, topped with cottage cheese and two or three peach slices
- bean sprouts, shredded carrot, cucumber strips and shredded lettuce topped with stir-fried chicken strips (seasoned during cooking with a little Chinese 5 spice powder) or marinated tofu
- lettuce, beetroot, tomato and orange segments topped with a little crumbled feta cheese
- lettuce, halved cherry tomatoes, grated carrot, thinly sliced radishes, topped with drained flaked tuna in water or brine

- a portion of cooked bulghar wheat with some flaked salmon, chopped roasted Mediterranean vegetables (peppers, courgette, mushrooms) and finely chopped spring onion
- a portion of cooked couscous with diced vegetables and stir-fried chicken
- a portion of brown rice with diced ham, pepper, cucumber, spring onion, pineapple and halved grapes
- a chicken or tuna and wholemeal pasta salad with diced tomatoes, pepper, cucumber, spring onions, sultanas and cashew nuts
- cold sliced new potatoes (cooked with their skins on to retain nutrients and fibre) – these make a tasty addition to a meal salad

Handy tip
On cold winter days a flask of homemade vegetable soup or spicy lentil soup, together with a wholemeal crusty roll, makes a satisfying lunch. It's also ideal for a weekend lunch (see the recipe on Page 96).

Healthy endings
Complete your lunch with a piece of fruit or a natural yoghurt with fruit. Lunch should always include at least one piece of fruit – it's an easy way to add to your target daily intake of three portions of fruit.

So what's a portion of fruit?
- a small bunch of grapes
- a satsuma, mandarin or clementine
- a small orange
- a medium apple
- a banana
- a pear
- a nectarine or peach
- a kiwi fruit
- a small carton or can of fruit in juice (remember to pack a spoon)
- a small pot of berry fruits (blueberries, strawberries, raspberries)
- a tablespoon of dried fruit (this counts only once per day)

Snack attack

Be ready for snack attacks – we all have them from time to time. If you devise your own list of simple healthy snacks, you'll be able to avoid diving for a chocolate bar or a doughnut.

Here are some ideas:
- a tablespoon of raisins or sultanas
- a yoghurt pot of plain popcorn – season it with some ground black pepper, a pinch of chilli or cayenne pepper if you like
- a slice of malt loaf
- a couple of large rice cakes, or a small packet of mini rice cakes
- a piece of fruit
- a bag or pot of veggie sticks – carrots, cucumber, celery, sweet pepper

Keep hydrated

Make sure you keep hydrated by drinking plenty of water or diluted fruit juice at lunchtime and through the day, particularly if you drink coffee or tea at your desk when you are working.

MAKING HEALTHY CHOICES

In the canteen

The secret of eating well in the staff canteen is to keep it simple. You may need to steer clear of the 'dish of the day', since this is often a fat-laden lasagne or a meat pie with a puff-pastry crust.

Go for:
● a bowl of soup and a crusty roll
● a jacket potato with a large salad – choose a healthy filling such as baked beans or tuna and give the cheese, coleslaw and mayonnaise-laced fillings a miss
● salmon or tuna salad
● pasta dishes with a tomato-based rather than a cream-based sauce
● a roast chicken (skin removed), lean ham, cottage cheese or prawn salad with a wholemeal roll

Try to find salads without creamy or oily dressings.

Avoid:
● anything that is fried, battered or crumbed
● pies, pasties and flans with pastry crusts
● anything with a creamy sauce
● creamy desserts

"Keep hydrated by drinking plenty of water or diluted fruit juice at lunchtime and through the day"

At the sandwich bar

If you buy your sandwich ready-made, always choose the healthy options and try to have wholemeal rather than white bread.

If sandwiches are made to order, go for the protein fillings that are served without dressing. This means giving the coronation chicken, prawn mayonnaise and egg mayonnaise a miss and settling instead for lean sliced ham, turkey, prawns, salmon or tuna without dressing. Make sure that your sandwich includes some salad vegetables and is well seasoned with pepper but not oversalted – go without salt if possible.

Keep an eye on the portion sizes – sandwiches from sandwich bars can be very generous.

At business lunches

If business lunches feature on your work programme, take care, or all your healthy good intentions could disappear. Keep these healthy-eating guidelines in mind and you'll be able to avoid piling in the calories.

- Choose a simple main course – a piece of grilled or baked fish or chicken without any creamy sauce, or go for a tomato-based pasta dish. Pile the vegetables high, but ask for them to be served without butter glazes. If there is a chance of a side salad, go for it – but ask for it with no dressing.
- Always restrict yourself to two courses. It's often a good idea to start with a soup or salad starter and to avoid temptation by not even *looking* at the dessert menu when it arrives! If you must have a dessert, choose a simple fruit sorbet or bowl of fresh-fruit salad.

● Give alcoholic drinks a miss at lunchtime and settle for fresh fruit juices or water.

CHILDREN'S LUNCHBOXES

Surveys of children's packed lunches have found that many children's lunchboxes are filled with chocolate bars, white-bread sandwiches, high-fat and high-salt processed snacks and fizzy drinks. You don't have to fall into this trap.

Providing a healthy lunchbox for your children is simple. It doesn't need to be time-consuming or break the bank. In fact, if you make the contents yourself they can look like the ready-prepared lunchbox food that fills the supermarket shelves but will cost you less and be far healthier. It's a sad fact that many of the prepared children's lunch foods are overprocessed and too high in fat, salt and sugar.

The most important things to remember when packing a child's lunchbox are that it needs to be nourishing and enjoyable – and, in their eyes, 'cool'.

Lunchbox lessons

● Try to keep children interested in lunch by ringing the changes.
● Don't be too adventurous – this isn't the time to introduce unfamiliar items. Try them out at home first.
● Make treats such as crisps and cakes occasional, and, when you do use them, try to select the healthier products.
● Let older children have some say in what goes into their lunchboxes – within your guidelines. Tell them what is available, and encourage them to get involved in the preparation. Persuade them to invent

their own fillings for sandwiches and wraps – it gives them a sense of responsibility and encourages them to make healthy choices for themselves. But be ready to offer guidance if their suggested combinations are too 'way out'.

● Don't worry if your child wants to eat the same filling in their sandwiches every day. It is more important that they *do* eat them. If their preference is for a filling that doesn't contain protein – even if it's something less desirable such as jam or honey – it's simple to provide some protein separately, such as stir-fried chicken strips, a couple of sticks of cheese, some cottage cheese and pineapple in a small pot, or a small yoghurt or fromage frais.

● Keep lunchbox food simple to eat with fingers or a spoon.

● The risk of being teased because they've got 'weird food' is a sure-fire discouragement to open their lunchbox in front of other children, so ensure that their healthy lunchbox food doesn't look too different from that of their friends.

● Avoid the morning rush by preparing lunchboxes the night before – then everyone can help. You can keep the lunches in the fridge until the morning.

Boxing clever

The next time you're in the supermarket, take a walk along the aisle of lunchbox foods aimed at children. You'll see that the food on offer is easy to make yourself at much less cost, and you'll know exactly what is in it. All you need is some lean sliced ham, chicken or cheese, some sliced granary or wholemeal bread or a few mini oatcakes or healthy crackers, to make your own construct-it-yourself 'lunch packs' like the ones you see in the shops.

With the help of a circular cutter – or the rim of a suitably sized cup or glass – you can easily reproduce your own circles of meat, cheese and bread (or you could cut them into squares or triangles). You can also make your own healthy dips and offer them with vegetable sticks and two or three breadsticks broken into shorter lengths. It's so easy.

Remember, if you do buy cooked meats, avoid the highly processed 're-formed' meats in favour of simple 'baked' or 'roasted' joints or cuts.

Lunchbox winners

When you're planning lunchboxes remember that in their lunchtime meal children need:

- protein
- carbohydrate
- calcium-rich food (usually dairy)
- fruit and vegetables
- a drink
- a treat

Here are just a few ideas to add variety to a child's lunchbox (you may even like to try some of them in your own).

Bread

Use wholemeal or granary bread if possible, but, if children say they don't like it, use one of the new high-fibre 'white' loaves. Or, if they are willing to compromise, try one slice of white (or high-fibre) bread and one slice of brown.

Vary the type of bread you use and try wraps, pittas, mini pittas, mini bagels or rolls. Experiment with some of the more exciting breads such as walnut bread, sun-dried-tomato bread, raisin or cheese bread – but give these a trial run at the weekend before adding them to the lunchbox, in case the child doesn't want to eat it.

Sandwich tips

- To avoid soggy sandwiches, dry any salad vegetables well after washing them.
- Go easy on the spread – you won't need any if the sandwich filling itself is moist.
- Keep sandwiches small – a 'doorstep' can look very intimidating, especially to a small child.

Here are some sandwich fillings they might like to try:

- low-fat soft cheese with finely sliced dried apricot or grated carrot
- roast chicken slices with a little cranberry sauce or homemade chutney
- crunchy peanut butter with cucumber slices

- slices of hardboiled egg with finely diced tomato (if you scrape out the seeds the filling will be less wet)
- low-fat soft cheese, sliced banana and a drizzle of runny honey

Try to include some salad vegetables in the sandwich or put a few in a small container if the children prefer – cherry tomatoes, a few slices of cucumber and a few Little Gem lettuce leaves are ideal. Or they might like a pot of raw veggies – carrot sticks, pepper strips, cucumber sticks, and mange tout or sugar-snap peas.

If children don't like fillings in their bread, try giving them a small wholemeal roll with a chicken drumstick and some cherry tomatoes, baby lettuce leaves and cucumber slices served separately.

Sandwich alternatives

Some children, particularly older ones, are willing to consider alternatives to sandwiches in their lunchboxes.

On cold days they might welcome some homemade soup in a flask plus a crusty wholemeal bread roll. Vegetable-and-lentil soup is quick, easy to make and filling. You can vary the vegetables you use to make the soup depending on what you have available.

On summer days they may like to take a pasta or rice salad made with some salad vegetables and chicken, tuna, sardines or mackerel.

A simple lunchtime soup

(serves 4)

1 carrot, finely diced

1 medium potato, peeled and diced

1 small leek, washed and finely sliced

A couple of broccoli florets or cauliflower florets

1 low-salt vegetable stock cube (or use vegetable bouillon powder)

900ml water

50g red lentils

Freshly ground black pepper

Place all of the prepared vegetables, and the remaining ingredients, in a large saucepan and bring to the boil. Skim off any foam and reduce heat. Simmer the soup for 20 minutes until the vegetables are tender.

Remove some of the cooked vegetables (about three heaped slotted spoonfuls) to a bowl. Pour the remainder of the soup into a blender and blend until almost smooth. Pour the blended soup and the reserved vegetables back into the saucepan. Reheat the soup and serve or put into a warmed vacuum flask. Serve with a piece of crusty wholemeal bread or a roll.

Handy Tip

Lentils (and other pulses) are a great source of low-fat protein, as well as being rich in fibre, which is good for your digestion and helps prevent clogging of your arteries.

"On cold days a flask of homemade soup and a crusty wholemeal roll makes a satisfying lunch"

Pizza time

Homemade pizza is a favourite with children. Prepare a large one together for the evening meal, letting the children choose some of the toppings, and save slices for their lunchboxes.

Make a thick tomato-and-vegetable sauce to spread over the base, then top with a selection of thinly chopped or sliced vegetables – peppers, tomato, mushrooms, courgettes, onion – plus some small pieces of chicken, ham or tuna, and a little crumbled mozzarella or grated half-fat cheese.

Fruit and vegetables

Children are more likely to eat fruit and vegetables in their lunchboxes if they are small and easy to eat. Try including one of these:

- a small apple
- an easy-peel clementine or satsuma
- low-fat dip and some vegetable sticks
- small packs of dried fruit
- a handful of sugar-snap peas
- a small fruit smoothie
- some cherry tomatoes
- a small pot of fruit in juice
- a pot of fresh fruit slices
- a handful of grapes
- 2 fresh apricots
- a halved kiwi fruit (don't forget to put a spoon in the lunchbox so they can eat it like a boiled egg)

Dairy and calcium rich foods

Include a low-fat dairy food, such as cheese, yoghurt, fromage frais or a calcium-enriched soya alternative in your child's lunchbox, to provide the calcium needed to build healthy bones.

Many of the yoghurts and types of fromage frais aimed at children can be high in sugar, colourings and other additives, so hunt out those that are as low in sugar and as 'natural' as possible. You could alternatively include a small bottle of drinking yoghurt or 3 tablespoons of cottage cheese with pineapple (in a small sealed container).

Remember that nuts (especially almonds), sesame seeds and tinned sardines and salmon (where the soft bones are eaten) are also sources of calcium.

Treats

Everyone likes a treat now and again, so there's no need to ban them from your children's lunchbox. Just limit them to healthy ones and replace the chocolate bars and cakes with:

- scones, currant buns or fruit bread
- malt loaf, oatcakes, healthy homemade flapjack, or a piece of healthy-recipe fruitcake
- a tablespoon of sultanas or raisins
- 4 unsulphured dried apricots or some dried mango slices
- a child-sized handful of mixed nuts and seeds
- a small yoghurt pot filled with plain popcorn
- some bagel crisps (see the recipe on Page 59)

If children are deprived of their favourite lunchbox treats, they'll probably just get them from friends, or from shops outside school. Try to stop them feeling deprived by allowing occasional special treats (say, once or twice a week) such as:

- a tablespoon of yoghurt-covered raisins
- a small packet of low-fat, low-salt crisps
- a small packet of pretzels
- a small shop-bought cake

Lunchbox baking

If you bake at home for lunchboxes, look for recipes that are lower in fat and add a little less sugar. You can often cut down on the sugar in a recipe if it includes fruit, or by adding a little mashed banana or apple or apricot purée to increase the sweet taste. Make your own low-fat and low-sugar muffins – you can reduce the sugar and use mashed banana to sweeten them.

If your children love all things chocolate, flavour your baking with drinking chocolate that is 70 per cent cocoa, to give a delicious chocolaty taste.

If you want to use jam in sandwiches or cakes, choose one with reduced sugar and as high a fruit content as possible.

Drinks

Avoid fizzy drinks (some can contain as much as 13 teaspoons of sugar in a single can) and include water, diluted fruit juice or semi-skimmed milk in the lunchbox.

Handy tip

Add an ice pack to the lunchbox to keep the food cool. If you choose sandwich fillings that can be frozen, you can take the sandwiches out of the freezer at breakfast time and they will gradually defrost during the morning.

Chapter Five
Let's celebrate!

you are™
what
you eat™

COPING WITH CHRISTMAS

Most of us eat and drink more than we should over the Christmas and New Year holiday, and then compound the assault on our bodies by lounging in front of the TV for hours on end.

It's not only the traditional Christmas feast that does the damage: it's the parties, the chocolates, the nuts, the nibbles and the alcohol as well.

But you can still enjoy the festive season without overindulging. Armed with some nutritional knowledge you can make Christmas healthy without taking the fun out of the festivities. The secret of a healthy Christmas is moderation not self-denial.

Festive fact

The average person eats a staggering 7,000 calories on Christmas Day – and it would take thirteen hours of running to burn them all off.

Survival tactics

You want to survive the hectic run-up to Christmas – and still have the energy to enjoy it? Here are some tips.

● Plan your healthy menus for Christmas Day and any other entertaining well ahead. Keep them simple and make as much use as you can of seasonal fruit and vegetables.

- Make a detailed shopping list. Consider booking a supermarket delivery at the beginning of December for some of the heavy items. Stock up on store-cupboard items early.
- Make the most of your freezer. Choose starters and desserts that can be made ahead and frozen. It will help to reduce the pressure on Christmas Day.
- Check that you've got all the table linen, china, cutlery and glasses you'll need.
- Buy the fresh fruit and vegetable as late as you can, so that they are at their peak of freshness and packed full of nutrients.
- Get other members of the family involved in the preparation. Delegate – there is no reason why you should do everything yourself.

CHRISTMAS DAY

Breakfast

Start your day with a simple, light but sustaining breakfast. Make sure that you include some protein, such as egg, yoghurt or milk, and some complex, starchy carbohydrate to keep your energy levels up. If you don't, you'll be tempted to tuck into the sweets, chocolates and biscuits to keep you going until lunchtime.

For a festive breakfast try:
- some defrosted frozen summer berries added to a bowl of wholemeal cereal with semiskimmed milk

- a scrambled egg on a slice of wholemeal toast
- a couple of Scotch pancakes (wholemeal if possible) with some crushed red berries and a drizzle of honey

Lunch

Keep control of the Christmas lunch by preparing as much as you can yourself rather than buying it ready made from the supermarket. That way you will be able to keep and eye on the fat, salt and sugar in the meal.

If 'turkey and all the trimmings' are on your Christmas menu, you'll be pleased to know that there are some easy ways to trim the fat and cut the calories – and no one will even notice.

- Roast the turkey on a rack so that the fat can drain off, and remove the skin before serving the meat on to the plates.
- Instead of chipolata sausages wrapped in streaky bacon, wrap ready-to-eat prunes in tiny strips of back bacon. Stretch the bacon rashers using the back of a knife and you'll make them go twice as far.
- Make your own stuffing using brown breadcrumbs, finely chopped onion and fresh herbs, bound together with egg. Avoid adding butter to the stuffing or dotting the top with tiny pieces of butter before putting the stuffing into the oven. Don't be tempted to make the stuffing into balls to fry them – pop them into the oven and bake them instead.
- Try making your bread sauce with wholemeal breadcrumbs or half wholemeal and half white. Use skimmed milk, and don't add cream. But remember to use plenty of pepper.

- If you use pan juices to make the gravy, ensure that you strain away all of the fat first. (It is better to make your own gravy, as most granules and ready-made gravies are high in salt and may contain trans (hydrogenated) fats.)

- Sweeten homemade cranberry sauce with honey, make it less sweet than you normally would. The sharpness will complement the rich food better.

- Serve just a few roast potatoes, and more steamed or boiled ones. Leave your roast potatoes into large chunks so they absorb less fat.

- Whatever people say about the 'crispiness' it's said to give, don't be tempted to use duck or goose fat to roast your potatoes. A light spray of olive oil is fine, but remember to keep turning them. Try not to roast potatoes alongside the turkey, or else they'll absorb its fat.

- Serve large quantities of freshly cooked vegetables. If you put different vegetables in separate dishes, you'll find your guests will put more on their plates, as they take some from each.

- If Christmas isn't Christmas without the pudding, have a small piece and forgo the cream and brandy butter in favour of quark flavoured with a little brandy, or a homemade fresh-orange-juice-and-whisky sauce.

- Make your mince pies lidless and with filo pastry, and moisten the leaves of pastry with egg white rather than melted butter.

- Make your own mincemeat without the suet – it doesn't need it. Simply chop half of the apple called for in the recipe, and stew the other half. Add this to the mincemeat when it is cold. This will keep the mincemeat moist while it is maturing.

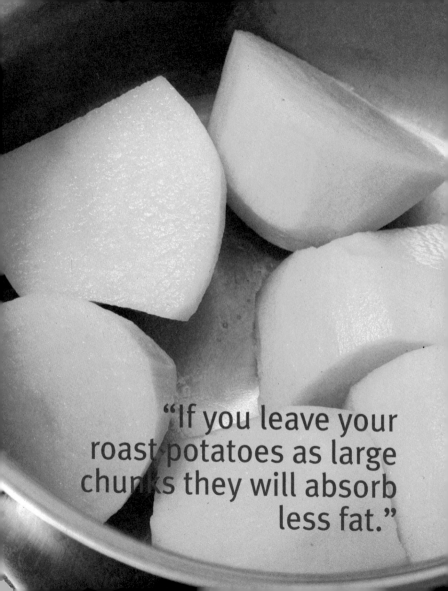

"If you leave your roast potatoes as large chunks they will absorb less fat."

Tea

Skip the traditional afternoon tea and go for a short walk instead. A cup of tea is fine at the end of the afternoon but, if you are planning a supper later in the evening, do you really need mince pies and Christmas cake now? Leave them for another day.

Supper

Christmas Day supper can be a delicious meal if you keep it simple and light.

A colourful array of salads with salsas and low-fat dressings and some cold meats are all that are needed to round off a perfect day. Instead of desserts, serve a tempting platter of fresh fruit.

Nifty nibbles

Instead of putting out bowls of crisps and salted peanuts for your guests (and for the family), fill the bowls with mixed nuts, raisins and seeds or pretzels, mini oatcakes, plain popcorn, or homemade garlic bagel crisps (see the recipe on Page 59).

PARTY TIME

Christmas and New Year parties can be a wobbly time if you're trying to eat healthily, what with all that freely flowing alcohol and fatty, salty snacks.

Some party food can be scarily high in fat, so knowing what to choose from an array of dishes on the buffet table or from the tempting canapés on offer makes good sense.

With the nutritional know-how you've gained from this book, you can make healthy choices – and still have a great time.

Enjoy the company and the surroundings and let food and drink play second fiddle. And, if you're the party host or hostess, there's no excuse not to get your New Year off to a healthy start.

Hosting the perfect party

With so much ready-made party food available in supermarkets at Christmas time, it's hardly surprising that busy hostesses make a dash to stock up their fridges and freezers. But, delicious though it may look, much of it is less than healthy, and a good proportion will have been fried, such as the mini versions of the Indian and Chinese starters we are all familiar with – the bhajis, samosas, pakoras and the prawn toasts and crispy wontons. But there are still some party timesavers that you can pick up from the supermarket – if you read the labels.

So, if you are buying ready-made for entertaining, opt for soft cheese wrapped in salmon, sushi, or low-fat dips that you can serve with crudités.

But, if you can, make time to prepare some homemade healthy canapés – your guests will be most impressed to be offered something fresh, tasty and, above all, different.

On the following page you'll find some ideas for simple canapés that won't break the calorie bank.

- Make bases for canapés using filo pastry. Cut small triangles of pastry and brush with lightly beaten egg white. Gently press three layers of pastry (each one at a 45-degree angle from the one below) into mini muffin cases and bake at 180°C/Gas 4 until golden and crispy.

- Make canapé bases by cutting circles from wholemeal bread or using thin slices of bagels, and baking them slowly in the oven. Pumpernickel and rye bread also make ideal bases for canapés.

- Add tasty low-fat toppings to pieces of vegetable. Try small pieces of cucumber with the seeds scooped out, halved cherry tomatoes, pieces of red pepper, small strips of celery or halved chicory leaves. Make sure that any filling you make is not too wet. Low-fat cream cheese makes an ideal filling. Give it more flavour by adding a little crushed garlic, finely chopped fresh herbs or chilli flakes.

- Lay a thin slice of lean ham on a board. Combine a little low-fat cheese with a squeeze of ready-made English mustard. Spread on to the ham and roll up. Cut the rolls into bite-sized pieces and secure with a cocktail stick. Thin slices of lean roast beef also work well, if you use low-fat soft cheese combined with horseradish sauce for spreading.

- Stir-fry strips of chicken with a little soy sauce or sweet chilli sauce. Serve with a low-fat-yoghurt-and-mint dip.

- Combine 2 tablespoons of finely chopped cucumber (seeds and skin removed) with a small tin of red salmon, a tablespoon of low-fat dressing, a pinch of chilli powder and black pepper. Put teaspoons of the mixture on chicory leaves or squares of rye bread.

- Combine low-fat cream cheese with a little drained and finely chopped pineapple and red pepper. Put a small teaspoonful of the mixture on healthy canapé bases such as mini oatcakes, or serve as a dip with vegetable sticks.

- Make cocktail pizzas. Slice a wholemeal baguette horizontally, and make a quick tomato topping by combining a small tin of tomatoes, a tablespoon of tomato purée, ½ teaspoon dried mixed herbs and a little freshly ground black pepper. Spread the topping on the baguette slices and top with small pieces of vegetable such as onion or sweet pepper chopped small. Grate over it a little half-fat strong cheese or mozzarella. Bake until the bread is crisp and the cheese is melted. Cut the pizza into 2cm strips and serve.

And for some really easy bites, try:
- cocktail oatcakes or water biscuits topped with low-fat soft cheese and a little smoked salmon
- pickled onions, gherkins and pineapple cubes speared on cocktail sticks – leave out the cheese
- a bowl of stuffed olives

Buffet survival

When you are faced with plates of delicious canapés and nibbles on a buffet table, here's how to keep on the nutritional straight and narrow without feeling deprived.

- Move away from the buffet table as soon as you've filled your plate. It'll reduce the temptation to stand and 'pick'.
- Pile your plate high with crudités and salad vegetables – even if they were intended as garnish!
- Don't imagine that small is always beautiful: one tiny vol-au-vent with a creamy rich filling can pack a hefty fat punch.
- Avoid anything deep-fried, in a creamy sauce or made with puff pastry.

- From a cold-meat platter, choose chicken or turkey (remove any skin), or lean ham. Give salami, liver sausage and other processed meats a miss.
- Fill your plate with salad and take only very small portions of creamy pasta dishes or curries.
- Studies have shown that we lose our inhibitions and eat more when the lights are turned down low, so gravitate to a well-lit part of the room.
- Skip the crisps, salted nuts and cheesy snacks.

Smart selections

Avoid	Choose
spring roll	piece of sushi
sausage roll	cocktail sausage (still high in fat, though)
piece of Stilton	piece of brie
slice of pizza	tomato-topped bruschetta
cream cheese dip	tomato salsa
prawn crackers	oatcakes
vol-au-vents	grilled prawns
chicken satay	veggie kebabs

Get active

There's so much more to Christmas time than eating and drinking.

- Switch off the TV and play charades, dominoes or pin the tail on the donkey. Get out a board game or a pack of cards.
- Put on some music and dance.
- Get out the holiday brochures and plan a holiday – or just dream.
- Take a trip to an ice rink – it's great exercise and fun.
- Book tickets for a panto – the laughing will do you a power of good.
- Wrap up warm and go for a walk – it'll help burn off those extra Christmas calories.

Recharge your batteries

Take time out for a nap – they're not just for toddlers. Twenty minutes' shuteye is all that's needed to make you feel refreshed and ready to start again.

Chocolates

If Christmas wouldn't be Christmas without chocolate, then treat yourself to a small box or bar of connoisseur chocolates made with good-quality ingredients and without hydrogenated (trans) fat or a whole list of E-numbers. Go for high cocoa solids chocolate – 70% or above is best. The higher the cocoa solids, the less room there is for sugar and fat, and the more intense the flavour.

"The recommended maximum intake of alcohol is two units per day for women and three for men"

Drink and be merry!

For many of us the festive season just wouldn't be festive without a little drink – or two, or more? The key word is 'little'. While a small glass of red wine every day or two can help prevent heart disease in some people, thanks to the polyphenols (plant chemicals) it contains, an alarming number of us find it difficult to stop at one small glass.

The recommended maximum intake of alcohol is two units per day for women and three for men, and you should also have two or three alcohol-free days each week. Binge drinking is especially harmful, so don't be tempted to save up your units for a big party!

And those units add up surprisingly quickly. Many people wrongly believe that a glass of wine equals a unit, simple as that. But that's a small glass of wine, not the large glasses that many pubs and restaurants now serve as standard, which can raise your tally to one and a half or even two units per glass.

Also, remember that drinks served at home tend to be more generous than pub measures, too, and cocktails may look innocent but can contain four or five units in a single drink!

What's a unit?
- Half a pint of average-strength beer, lager or cider (3–4% alcohol by volume, or ABV).
- A small glass of wine (9% alcohol by volume).

- A standard pub measure (25ml) of spirits (40% alcohol by volume).
- A standard pub measure (50ml) of fortified wine, e.g. sherry, port (20% alcohol by volume).

Cans of beer and lager often contain about three-quarters of a pint, rather than half, and so will contain 1.5 units – and more if it's a high-strength brew.

It's also easy to tot up two units in one drink. All of the following equal approximately two units:

- a pint (568ml) or a large can (say 500ml) of average-strength beer, lager or cider (3–4 per cent alcohol by volume)
- half a pint or half a large can of high-strength beer or lager (8 or 9 per cent alcohol by volume)
- a large (50ml) measure of spirits
- a large glass (175ml) of wine that is 11 or 12 per cent alcohol by volume
- a 330ml bottle of lager or alcopop (5.5 per cent alcohol by volume)

Another reason to beware the booze

Many people are surprised by how many calories there are in their drinks. A gram of alcohol contains seven calories. That's more than a gram of protein or carbohydrate – only fat has more!

So, it's surprisingly easy to pile on the pounds by knocking back a few drinks! Here are the calorie counts of a few popular tipples:

Favourite tipple	Calories
Beers, lager and cider (half pint)	
bitter	90
mild	71
pale ale	91
brown ale	80
stout	105
lager – ordinary strength	85
dry cider	95
sweet cider	110
Wine (small 125ml glass)	
red	85
rosé	89
white (sweet)	118
white (medium)	94
white (dry)	83
sparkling white	95

Fortified wine (50ml measure)	
port	79
sherry (dry)	58
Spirits (25ml pub measure)	
gin, vodka, whisky, brandy, rum etc.	52

Liqueurs, being so high in sugar, and sometimes cream as well, are the most calorific. And don't forget the mixers: juice such as orange, pineapple or grapefruit at least contains vitamins, but you still need to take the sugar and calorie count into account. And cola, lemonade and the like are basically sugar, fizzy water and flavourings. Choosing diet versions cuts the calories, but adds to your intake of potentially nasty additives in the form of artificial sweeteners. As for alcopops – don't even think about going there!

If you're going to drink ...
- Don't drink on an empty stomach.
- Go slowly – no more than one unit per hour.
- Alternate alcoholic drinks and nonalcoholic drinks or water. It'll slow down the amount you drink.
- Stick to one kind of drink.

Be kind to yourself

Most of us eat far too much at Christmas – and who enjoys the bloated feeling afterwards? But when all is said and done, Christmas and the New Year are about celebration.

What can you do – is there some kind of compromise?

You can – and should – do all you can to cut down your intake of the real 'baddies' that are full of fat, sugar and salt during the festive season. But you can still have fun and enjoy your food – you don't have to be a party pooper, or eat like a church mouse. Give yourself a treat and indulge yourself a little if you like – after all, it's only once a year!

If you do fall off the healthy-eating wagon over Christmas and the New Year, don't worry about it. You're only human, and it is the season of goodwill, after all. Don't go on a guilt trip. Forgive yourself, and simply start again where you left off. It's easy to undo a bit of nutritional naughtiness, by resolving to eat extra-healthily from now on.

Remember, tomorrow is a new day.

About the author

Nutrition consultant, author and journalist Carina Norris MSc (Dist.) RNutr studied biology followed by public-health nutrition. She was the nutritionist for Channel 4's *Turn Back Your Body Clock*, and has written several books on health and nutrition, including *You Are What You Eat: The Meal Planner That Will Change Your Life*, *Turn Back Your Body Clock* and *You Are What You Eat: Live Well, Live Longer*. She has co-authored *Lorraine Kelly's Junk-Free Children's Eating Plan* and *Is That My Child? The Brain Food Plan*. Carina is now working on a PhD on children's nutrient intake. She has a passion to spread the word on healthy twenty-first century living and help people de-junk their diets – the fun way.
(See www.carinanorris.co.uk.)

Index

additives 10, 15
adzuki beans 28
al fresco meals 79
alcohol 68, 91
  at festive season 115–18
  calorific value 117–18
  recommended maximum
    intake 115
  units 115–16
  alcopops 116
almonds 28
Alzheimer's Disease 8
anchovies 46
antibiotics, in food chain 10
apples
  buying 18
  dried 29
apricots, dried 29
asparagus 17
aspartame 37
autumn produce 27
avocados 12

Bagel crisps 59
baked beans 29, 34, 35
baking
  cakes and biscuits 33
  for lunchboxes 100
  meat, poultry and fish 42–4
bananas 18
barbecues 79
basil 28
beans 13, 15, 16, 28
  replacing meat with 32
  Tomato and mixed bean
    stew 45
  see also by type
beer 115, 116
  calorific value 117
berries, frozen 50
binge drinking 115

biscuits 16, 33
blackberries, frozen 50
blenders, stick 52
blood pressure, high 11
  and salt 13
blueberries
  dried 29
  frozen 50
boiling 46
bouillon powder 34
boxes, fruit and veg 25
brain, ageing and 8
Brazil nuts 28
bread
  for children's lunchboxes
    94
  freezing 51
  wholemeal 13, 16
bread sauce 105
breakfast
  all-day breakfasts 62
  Christmas Day 105–6
  importance of 9, 55
broccoli 48
'brown' foods 13
Brussels sprouts 48
buckwheat 13, 28
buffets 111–12
bulghar wheat 13, 28
bulkers 10
burger bars 63–4
burgers 32
  freezing 51
  homemade 75
business lunches 80
business travel 55
butchers 16
butter 16, 32, 67

cabbages 17
cafés 55, 62

caffeine 60
cakes 16, 33, 100
calcium 22, 99
calories 8, 23
  in alcohol 117–18
  Christmas Day consumption
    103
  in fats 11
  low-calorie products 22
  reduced-calorie products
    20, 22
canapés 108, 109–11
cancer 8, 11
cannellini beans 28
canola oil 12
canteens 7, 88
cappuccinos 60
carbohydrates, in fruit and
    vegetables 11
carrots 17, 46
cashew nuts 28
casseroling 45
cauliflowers 17
celebrations, survival of 7,
    103–19
celery 46
cereals, breakfast 20
  sugar content 34
cheese 16
  in children's lunchboxes 99
  on pizzas 76
  reduced-fat 33
cherries 18
chicken
  Chicken and pepper stir-fry
    40
  flavour boosters 46, 48
  Homemade chicken
    nuggets 77
  Mustard and honey chicken
    44

chickpeas 28
children, lunchboxes 91–101
Chinese food 71–2, 109
chips 16, 65
  homemade oven 75–6
chocolate 16, 35, 113
cholesterol
  and fats 11, 12, 21
  and wholefoods 13
Christmas 103–19
Christmas pudding 106
cider 115, 117
cinnamon 28
circulation 8
cocktails 115
coconut oil 11
coffee 60
coffee bars 60
colourants 15
cooking
  food from scratch 10
  salt added during 34
cooking methods
  healthy 7, 39
  reduced-fat 32
  see also under individual
    methods
corn oil 11, 12, 39
cornflour 28
cottage cheese 99
courgettes 17
couscous 28
cranberries, dried 29
cranberry sauce 106
cream 33
crisps 16
  Bagel crisps 59
cucumbers 17
currant buns 13, 57
currants 29
curry powder 28

dairy produce
  in children's lunchboxes 99
  fat content 11
  healthy choices 16
deep fat fryers 11, 39
dehydration 9, 90
department stores, cafés 62
desserts 35
'diet' drinks 35, 64
dried food, storage 30
dried fruit 29, 89
  in children's lunchboxes 99
  Energy bars 58–9
drinks
  alcoholic 68, 91, 115–18
  best 9, 35
  in children's lunchboxes
    100
  in fast-food chains 64
dry frying 39
duck fat 106

E-numbers 15, 23
eating out 7, 55–79
eggs
  antibiotics and growth
    promoters in 10
  saturated fat in 11
electric health grills 49, 51
Energy bars 58–9
energy levels 8
  and sugar consumption 12
equipment, kitchen 49, 51–2
European Union, legislation
  on food labelling 21–2
evaporated milk 33
exercise 113

fajita wraps 56
farm shops 10, 15
farmers' markets 10, 15

fast-food chains 63–4
fats
  amount per 100g 21
  cutting down on 32–3
  good and bad 11–12
  low fat foods 23
  in processed food 8, 9, 10,
    15
  reduced-fat foods 22
fibre
  in fruit and vegetables 11
  high fibre foods 23
  soluble 13
figs, dried 29
fillers 10
filo pastry 33, 106, 110
fish
  Baked cod with
    Mediterranean topping 44
  in diet 32
  homemade fish and chips
    75–6
  oily 12, 16
  preparing 49
fish-and-chip shops 65
fishmongers 16
five a day 11
fizzy drinks 9, 35, 64
flavour boosters 46–8
flour 28
food choices 7
food manufacturers, health
  claims by 21–2
food processors 49
food safety 56, 79, 84, 101
Food Standards Agency 20
foreign food 70–4, 77
freezers 50–1
freshness, and nutrient
  content 10
fromage frais 16

in children's lunchboxes 99
frozen foods 25
  for lunchboxes 101
fructose 37
fruit 8, 9
  buying 15, 18
  canned 35, 87
  in children's lunchboxes 98
  freshness of 10
  health benefits 11
  organic 10
  in packed lunches 86–7
  portions 87
  as snacks 57
fruit juice 9, 29, 88, 91
fruit spreads 34
fruit tea 9
frying 11
  best oils for 12

gadgets 51–2
garlic 46
ginger 28, 48
goose fat 106
grains 28
grapes 18
gravy 106
green beans 17
grilling 39, 46
grills, electric health 49, 51
groundnut oil 39
growth promoters, in food
  chain 10

hair 8
hazelnuts 28
health claims 21–2
healthy eating, benefits of 8
heart disease 8, 11, 12, 21
herbs 28, 34
  freezing 50

storage 30
high fibre products 23
holidays, healthy eating on
  77–9
homegrown produce 10, 15
honey
  Energy bars 58–9
  Mustard and honey chicken
    44
hunger, and shopping 25
hydrogenated fats
  avoiding 32
  harmful effects of 12, 21
  in processed food 10, 15

Indian food 70–1, 109
Italian food 73–4

jams, reduced-sugar 34, 100
junk food 8, 9, 27

kidney beans 28
kilocalories see calories
knives 51

labels 7
  checking when shopping
    15, 49
  health claims on 21–2
  reading 20–4
labour-saving devices 49,
  51–2
lactose 37
lager 115, 116, 117
lamb, Lamb chops with
  crumb and mint crust 42
lattes 60
leftovers 82–4
lemons 18, 46
lentils 13, 16, 28
  A simple lunchtime soup 96

lettuces 17
lifestyle, 10 tips for healthier
  9–13
liqueurs 118
liquidisers 52
lists, shopping 24–5
  for Christmas 104
  on holiday 78
longevity 8
low fat products 23, 35
low sodium/low salt
  products 23, 34
low-calorie products 22
low-sugar products 22, 24
lunch
  Christmas 105–6
  importance of 81
  packed 7, 55–6, 81–7,
    91–101

malt loaf 89
markets 15, 77, 78
marrows 17
meat
  antibiotics and growth
    promoters in 10
  fat content 11
  healthy choices 16
  processed and re-formed
    93, 112
  reducing quantity in diet 32
Mediterranean diet 73
melons 18
menus
  choosing healthy options
    · from 67–9
  planning 24, 49
milk
  antibiotics and growth
    promoters in 10
  skimmed 16, 32

milk shakes 64
millet 13, 28
mince pies 106
minerals, in fruit and
    vegetables 11
minor illnesses 8
mint 28
    Lamb chops with crumb
    and mint crust 42
mixers 118
money-off vouchers 25
monounsaturated fats 11, 12
mood 12
motorway service stations
    55, 62
muesli 34
muffins 60
    homemade 100
mushrooms 17
mushroom omelette 48
Mustard and honey chicken
    44

naps 113
natural sugars 13, 20, 37
New Year 103, 108
nibbles, Christmas 108
no added sugar products
    20, 22
nutmeg 48
nutrients, on labels 20
nuts 12, 16, 28
    Energy bars 58–9
    see also by type

oatcakes 58
oats 28
    Energy bars 58–9
obesity 12
oils
    choice of 11, 12

spraying 32, 46
for stir-frying 39
storage 30
olive oil 11, 12
omega-3 12
omega-6 12
omelette, mushroom 48
onions 17
online shopping 25
orange juice 46, 50
oranges 18
organic food 10
    fruit and veg boxes 25
oven chips 75–6
own-brand products 25

packed lunches 7, 55–6
    for adults 81–7
    for children 91–101
palm oil 11
parsley 50
parties 108–12
pasta 73–4
    wholemeal 13, 16, 27
pastry 33, 106
peaches, dried 29
peanut butter 34
peanut oil 12
pears, dried 29
peppers
    Baked cod with
    Mediterranean topping 44
    Chicken and pepper stir-fry
    40
pesticides, in food chain 10
phytochemicals, in fruit and
    vegetables 11
picnics 55
pie fillings 51
pine nuts 28
pineapples 18

pitta pockets 56
pizza
    choice of 73
    cocktail pizzas 111
    homemade 76
    in lunchboxes 98
pizza places 63
poaching 39, 45
polyphenols 115
polyunsaturated fats 11, 12
popcorn 33, 35, 57, 87
port 116, 118
potatoes 17
    oven chips 75–6
    roast 106
prawns
    frozen 51
    Simple hot and spicy prawn
    and tomato stir-fry 41
preparation, food 10
preservatives 20
processed food 8, 9
    ditching habit of 10, 16
    hydrogenated fats in 12
salt in 13, 33
protein
in beans and lentils 13
in children's lunchboxes 92
prune juice 46
prunes 29, 105
pub grub 65
puff pastry 111
pulses 13, 15, 16, 29
pumpkin seeds 28, 48

quark 106
quinoa 13

raisins 29
rapeseed oil 11
raspberries 50

ready meals 16, 33, 49
reduced-calorie products 20, 22
reduced-fat products 22
reduced-sugar products 22, 34
restaurants 67–9
rice, brown 13, 16, 27, 28
rice cakes 87
rice flour 28
risotto 74
roasting 42–4
rosemary 46, 50

saccharine 37
safflower oil 12
sage 50
salad dressings 33, 67
salads, lunchbox 85–6
salmon 48
salt
  amount per 100g 21
  cutting down on 33–4
  low salt foods 23
  maximum recommended daily intake 24
  in processed food 10, 15, 24
  reading labels for 24
  reducing intake 13
  very low salt foods 23
sandwich bars 90
sandwiches
  for children's lunchboxes 94–5
  for packed lunches 56, 84–5
  shop-bought 57, 90
  toasted 52
saturated fats 11
  in processed food 10, 15
  replacing with unsaturated 32

saucepans 51
sauces
  basic stir-fry 40
  freezing 50
sausages 32, 73, 74, 105
scones 13, 57
seasonal produce 10, 25, 26–7
seeds 12, 16, 28
  Energy bars 58–9
self-catering holidays 78–9
sell-by dates 10, 15
sesame seeds 28, 48
sherry 116, 118
shopping 7, 15–37
  clever tips for 24–5
  for freshness 10
  healthy 7, 15–16
  and stress 24
skin 8
smoothie makers 49
snacks
  Christmas Day 108
  healthy 57, 87
  homemade 33
  low-sugar 35
  sugary and fatty 8
sodium
  amount per 100g 21
  low sodium foods 23
  reading labels for salt 24
  very low sodium foods 23
  see also salt
sorbitol 37
soups 33
  A simple lunchtime soup 96
  for packed lunches 86, 95
source of fibre products 23
soy sauce 34, 40
spaghetti, tinned 34, 35
Spanish food 74

spices 28, 34
storage 30
spinach 48
spirits 116, 118
spring produce 26
squash, fruit 9, 35
steamers 52
steaming 39, 46
stewing 45
stick blenders 52
stir-fry sauce, basic 40
stir-frying 11, 39
  recipes 40–1
stock cubes 34
storage, canned and dried food 30
store cupboard, healthy 27–9
strawberries 18
stress
  at Christmas 103–4
  and cooking 7, 49
  and shopping 24–5
stroke 8, 11
stuffing 105
sugar
  amount per 100g 21
  cutting down on 12–13, 34–5
  in drinks 9
  hidden 35
  low sugar foods 20, 22
  natural 13, 20, 37
  no added sugar foods 20, 22
  in processed food 8, 9, 10, 15
  types of 37
sultanas 29
summer produce 26
sunflower oil 11, 12
sunflower seeds 28, 48

supermarkets
  cafés 62
  lunchbox foods 92
  own-brand products 25
  party food 109
supper, Christmas Day 108
sweetcorn 29
sweeteners, artificial
  in drinks 9
  in food 20
  safety of 37
sweets 16

takeaways 34, 70–4
  homemade 75–7
tap water 79
tea 60
tea, Christmas Day 108
teeth, and sugar 12
Thai food 72
tinned foods 29
  storage 30
toasted sandwiches 52
toasters 51
tomatoes 17
  Simple hot and spicy prawn
    and tomato stir-fry 41
  Tomato and mixed bean
    stew 45
trans fats see hydrogenated
    fats
travelling, on business 55
treats, in children's
    lunchboxes 99–100
tuna 48
turkey, Christmas 105
twenty-minute feasts 48

units, alcohol 115–16

vegetables 8, 9
  A simple lunchtime soup 96
  buying 15, 17
  canned 34
  in children's lunchboxes 98
  freshness of 10
  health benefits 11
  organic 10
  as snacks 58, 87
vegetarian options 67
very low sodium/very low
    salt products 23
vitamins
  in breakfast cereals 20
  and freshness 10
  in fruit and vegetables 11

walnuts 28, 46
water 9, 35, 90
  safety of 79
water chestnuts, Simple
    hot and spicy prawn and
    tomato stir-fry 41
weaning, adult 32–5
weight gain and loss 8
'white' foods 13
wholefoods 8, 9
  increasing consumption of
    13
wholemeal flour 28
wholemeal foods 13, 16, 27
wine 115
  calorific value 117
  fortified 116
winter produce 27
World Health Organisation 11

yoghurt 16
  in children's lunchboxes 99
  drinks 22
  low-fat 33
  in packed lunches 86